# RESPONSIVE WEB DESIGN WITH HTML5 AND CSS3

A Beginner's Guide

THOMPSON CARTER

# TABLE OF CONTENTS

# INTRODUCTION

## Responsive Web Design with HTML5 and CSS3: A Beginner's Guide"

The internet is no longer a single-device experience. People interact with websites on an ever-growing variety of devices— smartphones, tablets, laptops, desktops, smart TVs, and even wearable tech. This shift has revolutionized how websites are designed, bringing responsive web design (RWD) to the forefront. Responsive web design isn't just a trend; it's a necessity in today's interconnected digital world.

This book, *Responsive Web Design with HTML5 and CSS3: A Beginner's Guide,* is a comprehensive exploration of the principles, techniques, and tools you need to master the art of building responsive websites. Whether you're completely new to web design or looking to refine your skills, this book is designed to be a practical, jargon-free guide to understanding and applying responsive design principles in real-world projects.

### The Changing Landscape of Web Design

In the early days of the internet, web pages were static and primarily viewed on desktop computers with a limited range of screen sizes. Designers could comfortably create fixed-width layouts that worked across most devices. However, as technology evolved, mobile phones and tablets became the dominant means of accessing the web. This diversity in device sizes and resolutions made fixed layouts obsolete, ushering in the era of responsive web design.

Responsive design solves the challenges of creating websites that work seamlessly across devices with different screen sizes and capabilities. It ensures that content remains accessible, visually appealing, and functional, whether viewed on a 4-inch smartphone or a 65-inch 4K television. At its core, responsive web design is about flexibility—adapting your content to fit the context in which it's viewed.

## What You Will Learn

This book is organized to take you step-by-step through the fundamentals of responsive design, from the basics of HTML5 and CSS3 to advanced techniques like grid systems, animations, and performance optimization. Each chapter builds on the previous one, culminating in practical examples and real-world projects.

Here's what you can expect:

### 1. Foundations of Responsive Web Design

We'll start with the basics—what responsive web design is and why it's essential. You'll learn the principles of mobile-first design, how to approach designing for a range of devices, and why flexible grids, images, and media queries are the foundation of responsive layouts. By the end of this section, you'll understand the philosophy behind responsive design and how to begin applying it to your projects.

## 2. Core Technologies: HTML5 and CSS3

Before diving into responsive techniques, it's crucial to have a strong grasp of the core building blocks of web design: HTML5 and CSS3. You'll learn about semantic HTML elements like <header>, <main>, and <footer>, which improve accessibility and structure. CSS3 introduces powerful tools like Flexbox and Grid, which make creating flexible and responsive layouts intuitive. We'll also explore essential CSS properties, selectors, and techniques that you'll use throughout your responsive design journey.

## 3. Responsive Layout Techniques

At the heart of responsive design are layouts that adapt to various screen sizes. You'll learn:

- How to use **media queries** to apply styles based on device characteristics.
- The **CSS Flexbox layout**, ideal for creating responsive navigation bars and aligning elements.
- The **CSS Grid layout**, perfect for complex multi-column layouts and designing page structures that respond dynamically to screen size. These techniques will empower you to build layouts that are as functional as they are visually appealing.

## 4. Advanced CSS Techniques

To take your designs to the next level, we'll explore advanced CSS features:

- **CSS transitions and animations** to add interactivity and polish to your designs.
- **CSS variables** for maintaining consistent themes and easily customizable stylesheets.
- **Modern CSS properties** like clip-path and filter, which allow for cutting-edge design effects. These techniques will help you create professional, high-quality web pages that stand out.

## 5. Responsive Components

Beyond layouts, individual components like forms, buttons, and navigation menus must also adapt to various devices. You'll learn how to:

- Build **responsive forms** that are both accessible and user-friendly.
- Create **flexible navigation menus**, including hamburger menus for mobile devices.
- Use **media queries** and CSS utilities to ensure that every component on your page is optimized for the user's device.

## 6. Frameworks and Tools

Frameworks like Bootstrap and Tailwind CSS provide pre-built components and layouts, speeding up development without sacrificing flexibility. This book will guide you through:

- Setting up and using popular frameworks.
- Customizing frameworks to suit your design needs.
- Creating responsive layouts with minimal effort while maintaining a professional aesthetic.

## 7. Performance Optimization

Responsive websites must be fast. A slow website can lead to poor user experiences and lower search engine rankings. You'll learn:

- How to **optimize images and fonts** for faster load times.
- The benefits of using a **Content Delivery Network (CDN)**.
- Techniques for minifying CSS, HTML, and JavaScript to reduce file sizes. You'll also explore tools like Google Lighthouse to audit and improve your website's performance.

## 8. Accessibility in Responsive Design

A truly responsive website isn't just one that works on different devices—it's one that works for everyone. Accessibility ensures that your designs are usable by people with disabilities. We'll cover:

- The principles of web accessibility based on **WCAG guidelines**.
- Using **semantic HTML** and ARIA roles to improve screen reader compatibility.
- Testing tools and best practices to ensure inclusivity. This section will help you design websites that are not only beautiful and functional but also equitable.

### *9. Emerging Trends and Future of Responsive Design*

Web design is an ever-evolving field. This book concludes with a look at emerging technologies and techniques that will shape the future:

- **CSS Houdini** for extending CSS capabilities.
- **Container queries**, a game-changing addition to responsive design.
- **Design systems** for scalable and consistent designs in large projects. We'll also provide tips for staying updated with the latest trends in web design.

### Who Is This Book For?

This book is for:

- **Beginners**: If you're new to web design, this book provides a solid foundation in HTML5, CSS3, and responsive design principles.

- **Developers**: If you already have web development experience, you'll find advanced techniques and tools to take your skills to the next level.
- **Designers**: Learn how to create visually stunning and functional designs that work seamlessly on any device.

No matter your background, this book will help you confidently build responsive websites that meet the demands of today's multi-device web.

## Practical and Project-Based Learning

Throughout the book, we'll focus on hands-on learning with real-world examples. You'll build:

- A responsive blog layout.
- A modern, mobile-friendly navigation menu.
- A fully responsive e-commerce product page.
- A complete portfolio website that showcases your responsive design skills.

By the end of this book, you won't just understand responsive design—you'll have the tools and experience to create websites that are ready for the future.

Responsive web design isn't just a skill; it's a mindset. It's about anticipating the needs of users and delivering experiences that adapt to their devices and contexts. As you work through this book, you'll develop a deep understanding of how to build responsive, accessible, and high-performance websites that meet the challenges of today's web. Let's get started!

# CHAPTER 1: INTRODUCTION TO RESPONSIVE WEB DESIGN

In today's digital world, where users interact with websites across a myriad of devices, from smartphones to large desktop screens, the importance of responsive web design cannot be overstated. This chapter introduces the core concepts of responsive web design, explains why a mobile-first approach is essential, provides an overview of key tools and technologies, and compares responsive and non-responsive websites through a practical example.

**What is Responsive Web Design?**

Responsive web design (RWD) is a design approach that ensures websites deliver an optimal user experience across devices of various sizes and resolutions. A responsive website dynamically adjusts its layout, content, and functionality based on the device being used to view it.

*Key Features of Responsive Web Design:*

1. **Fluid Layouts**:
   o Elements resize proportionally using relative units (e.g., percentages) instead of fixed units (e.g., pixels).
2. **Media Queries**:

    o   CSS rules that apply styles based on the device's screen size, resolution, orientation, and other characteristics.

3. **Flexible Media**:

    o   Images, videos, and other media scale appropriately within their containers.

*Why Responsive Web Design Matters:*

1. **Device Diversity**:

    o   With the explosion of mobile devices, tablets, smart TVs, and desktops, users access the web in countless ways.

    o   Stat: Over 50% of global web traffic now comes from mobile devices.

2. **Improved User Experience**:

    o   A responsive website provides seamless navigation and readability without zooming, panning, or horizontal scrolling.

3. **SEO Benefits**:

    o   Search engines like Google prioritize responsive websites in mobile search results.

4. **Cost Efficiency**:

- o Instead of maintaining separate sites for mobile and desktop, a single responsive design serves all users.

## Importance of Mobile-First Design in the Modern Web

Mobile-first design flips the traditional design process by prioritizing mobile users first. This approach acknowledges the dominance of mobile web traffic and ensures a robust foundation for smaller screens, which can then scale up for larger devices.

### *Why Mobile-First Design?*

1. **Resource Optimization**:
   - o Focuses on the most critical content and features, eliminating unnecessary elements.
2. **Faster Load Times**:
   - o Lightweight designs optimized for mobile reduce page load times.
3. **Enhanced Accessibility**:
   - o Ensures that even users with slower internet connections or older devices can access the website.

### *Principles of Mobile-First Design:*

- **Progressive Enhancement**:
  - o Start with a basic design for mobile and add enhancements for larger devices.

- **Simplified Navigation**:
  - o Use compact menus (e.g., hamburger icons) and prioritize key actions.
- **Touch-Friendly Elements**:
  - o Buttons, links, and forms should be easy to interact with on touchscreens.

## Overview of Tools and Technologies

Responsive web design relies on foundational web technologies and tools that enable developers to create adaptive and flexible designs.

### 1. HTML5

HTML5 provides the structural backbone of responsive websites with features such as:

- **Semantic Elements**:
  - o <header>, <nav>, <article>, <section>, and <footer> improve content organization.
- **Media Support**:
  - o <picture> and <video> tags make handling responsive media simpler.

### 2. CSS3

CSS3 adds the styling capabilities needed for responsive design:

- **Media Queries**:
    - Introduced in CSS3, these allow conditional styling based on device characteristics.
- **Flexbox and Grid Layouts**:
    - Tools for creating flexible, responsive layouts.
- **Transitions and Animations**:
    - Enhance the user experience with subtle effects.

### 3. Media Queries

Media queries are a CSS feature that applies styles based on specific device properties like width, height, resolution, and orientation.

**Example**:

css
Copy code
```
/* Default styles for mobile */
body {
  font-size: 16px;
}

/* Styles for devices wider than 768px */
@media (min-width: 768px) {
  body {
```

```
  font-size: 18px;
 }
}
```

## 4. Tools for Development

- **Code Editors**:
    - o VS Code, Sublime Text, or Atom for writing HTML and CSS.
- **Browser Developer Tools**:
    - o Inspect layouts and simulate different screen sizes directly in browsers.
- **Frameworks**:
    - o Bootstrap and Tailwind CSS accelerate development with pre-built responsive components.

**Real-World Example: Comparing Responsive and Non-Responsive Websites**

To illustrate the power of responsive design, let's compare two websites—a non-responsive and a responsive version—when viewed on a smartphone:

*Non-Responsive Website:*

1. **Appearance**:

- o Content appears zoomed out, requiring users to pinch and zoom.
- o Horizontal scrolling is necessary to read text or view images.
- o Navigation menus are difficult to interact with on small screens.

2. **User Experience**:
   - o Frustrating and cumbersome, leading to high bounce rates.

### *Responsive Website:*

1. **Appearance**:
   - o The layout adjusts to fit the screen size, ensuring all content is legible.
   - o Images scale proportionally, avoiding distortion or overflow.
   - o Navigation is touch-friendly, with collapsible menus for smaller screens.

2. **User Experience**:
   - o Seamless and engaging, encouraging users to stay longer and explore more.

**Implementation Example**: Let's create a simple webpage to demonstrate responsive design:

**HTML**:

html
Copy code

```
<!DOCTYPE html>
<html lang="en">
<head>
  <meta charset="UTF-8">
  <meta name="viewport" content="width=device-width, initial-scale=1.0">
  <title>Responsive Example</title>
  <link rel="stylesheet" href="styles.css">
</head>
<body>
  <header>
    <h1>Welcome to My Responsive Website</h1>
  </header>
  <main>
    <p>This is a demo of responsive design principles.</p>
  </main>
</body>
</html>
```

**CSS**:

css

Copy code

```css
/* Default styles for mobile */
body {
  font-family: Arial, sans-serif;
  margin: 0;
  padding: 1em;
}

header h1 {
  font-size: 1.5em;
  text-align: center;
}

/* Styles for larger screens */
@media (min-width: 768px) {
  body {
    padding: 2em;
  }

  header h1 {
    font-size: 2.5em;
  }
}
```

1. Responsive web design ensures websites look and function well on all devices, enhancing user experience and accessibility.
2. A mobile-first approach prioritizes lightweight, touch-friendly designs that scale up gracefully.
3. Tools like HTML5, CSS3, and media queries are the foundation of responsive design.
4. Real-world comparisons highlight the practical benefits of adopting responsive web design.

In the next chapter, we'll dive into setting up your development environment, ensuring you're equipped with the tools needed to start building responsive websites. Let's get started!

# CHAPTER 2: SETTING UP YOUR DEVELOPMENT ENVIRONMENT

Before diving into responsive web design, it's crucial to establish a robust development environment. A well-configured setup ensures you can write, test, and debug your code efficiently. This chapter covers the installation of essential tools, setting up a local development server, exploring browser developer tools, and creating a project folder structure for a responsive website.

**Installing a Code Editor**

A code editor is your primary tool for writing HTML, CSS, and JavaScript. While many editors are available, **Visual Studio Code (VS Code)** and **Sublime Text** are among the most popular due to their versatility and support for web development.

*Why Choose VS Code?*

1. **User-Friendly Interface**:
   o Clean layout with customizable themes.
2. **Extensions**:
   o Thousands of plugins for productivity, such as live server integration and syntax highlighting.
3. **Integrated Terminal**:
   o Run commands directly within the editor.

4. **Built-in Git Support**:

   o   Manage version control without leaving the editor.

## *Installing VS Code*

1. **Download and Install**:

   o   Go to the VS Code website and download the version for your operating system.

   o   Follow the installation wizard to complete the process.

2. **Install Extensions**:

   o   Open VS Code and navigate to the **Extensions Marketplace**.

   o   Search for and install:

      ▪   **Live Server**: For a local development server.

      ▪   **Prettier**: For code formatting.

## *Why Choose Sublime Text?*

1. **Lightweight and Fast**:

   o   Minimal resource consumption, ideal for slower systems.

2. **Customizable**:

   o   Supports plugins and themes via the Package Control system.

## *Installing Sublime Text*

1.  **Download and Install**:
    - Visit the Sublime Text website and download the installer.

2.  **Set Up Package Control**:
    - Open the command palette (Ctrl+Shift+P or Cmd+Shift+P) and type "Install Package Control."
    - Use Package Control to install plugins like **Emmet** for faster HTML and CSS coding.

## Setting Up a Simple Local Development Server

A local development server allows you to view and test your website in a browser, reflecting changes in real-time without manual refreshing.

### *Using Live Server with VS Code*

1.  **Install Live Server**:
    - Go to the **Extensions Marketplace** in VS Code.
    - Search for and install the **Live Server** extension.

2.  **Run the Server**:
    - Open your project folder in VS Code.
    - Right-click the main HTML file in the file explorer.
    - Select **Open with Live Server**.

o The browser will automatically display your page, refreshing with every saved change.

### *Using Python's HTTP Server (Optional)*

If you prefer not to use VS Code or Live Server, Python provides a lightweight solution:

1. **Ensure Python is Installed**:
   - o Open a terminal and type python --version. If not installed, download it from the Python website.
2. **Start the Server**:
   - o Navigate to your project folder in the terminal.
   - o Run the command:

   bash
   Copy code
   python -m http.server 8000

   - o Open http://localhost:8000 in your browser to view the website.

### Introduction to Browser Developer Tools

Browser developer tools are essential for debugging and refining responsive websites. Most modern browsers, including Chrome, Firefox, and Edge, provide powerful developer tools.

### *Accessing Developer Tools*

1. Open your website in a browser.

2. Right-click anywhere on the page and select **Inspect** or press F12.

### *Key Features of Developer Tools*

1. **Elements Panel**:
   - View and edit HTML and CSS in real-time.
   - Example: Modify font size or color directly in the browser to test design changes.

2. **Console Panel**:
   - Debug JavaScript errors and execute scripts.
   - Example: Check if a media query is triggering correctly.

3. **Network Panel**:
   - Monitor network requests and performance.
   - Example: Identify large images slowing down page load times.

4. **Device Mode**:
   - Simulate different screen sizes and resolutions.
   - Click the **Toggle Device Toolbar** icon to test your responsive design on various devices like smartphones and tablets.

**Real-World Example: Configuring a Project Folder Structure**

A well-organized project folder structure ensures maintainability and scalability as your website grows. Here's a simple structure for a responsive website project:

*Folder Structure*

Copy code

```
responsive-website/
├── index.html
├── css/
│   └── styles.css
├── js/
│   └── script.js
├── images/
│   └── logo.png
└── README.md
```

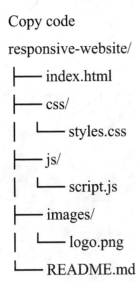

*Description of Files and Folders*

1. **index.html**:
   - The main HTML file that serves as the entry point for the website.
2. **css/ Folder**:
   - Contains all CSS files for styling the website.
   - Example File: styles.css for main styles.
3. **js/ Folder**:

- o Contains JavaScript files for interactivity.
4. **images/ Folder**:
    - o Stores all media assets, such as logos and background images.
5. **README.md**:
    - o A markdown file for documenting project details, such as purpose and setup instructions.

### *Building a Simple Project*

Let's create a basic HTML file with linked CSS and JavaScript:

**HTML (index.html)**:

html
Copy code

```
<!DOCTYPE html>
<html lang="en">
<head>
  <meta charset="UTF-8">
  <meta name="viewport" content="width=device-width, initial-scale=1.0">
  <title>Responsive Website</title>
  <link rel="stylesheet" href="css/styles.css">
</head>
<body>
  <header>
    <h1>Welcome to My Responsive Website</h1>
```

```
 </header>
 <script src="js/script.js"></script>
</body>
</html>
```

**CSS (css/styles.css)**:

```css
css
Copy code
body {
  font-family: Arial, sans-serif;
  margin: 0;
  padding: 0;
  text-align: center;
}

header {
  background-color: #007bff;
  color: white;
  padding: 1em 0;
}
```

**JavaScript (js/script.js)**:

```javascript
javascript
Copy code
console.log('Welcome to my responsive website!');
```

***Previewing the Website***

- Open the project folder in your code editor.
- Use Live Server or Python's HTTP server to launch the site.
- Experiment with resizing the browser and toggling device mode to see how the layout adapts.

1. **Tools Matter**:
   - A good code editor like VS Code or Sublime Text can significantly enhance productivity.
2. **Local Server is Essential**:
   - Real-time previews with tools like Live Server speed up the development process.
3. **Developer Tools are Your Friend**:
   - Debugging and testing designs across devices is critical for responsive web development.
4. **Organized Projects Save Time**:
   - A structured folder layout ensures easier collaboration and maintenance.

In the next chapter, we'll dive into the **basics of HTML5**, setting the foundation for building structured and semantic web pages. Let's get started!

# CHAPTER 3: BASICS OF HTML5

HTML5 is the foundation of every web page. It provides the structure that browsers interpret and display to users. In this chapter, we'll explore the HTML5 document structure, cover essential HTML elements, understand the importance of semantic HTML, and build a real-world example—a blog homepage.

## Understanding the HTML5 Document Structure

An HTML document starts with a structured outline that ensures browsers and search engines can properly interpret its content.

### *Basic HTML5 Skeleton*

Here's the structure of a simple HTML5 document:

```
html
Copy code
<!DOCTYPE html>
<html lang="en">
<head>
  <meta charset="UTF-8">
  <meta name="viewport" content="width=device-width, initial-scale=1.0">
  <title>My First HTML Page</title>
</head>
<body>
```

```
<h1>Welcome to My Website</h1>
</body>
</html>
```

## *Key Elements in the Structure*

1. **<!DOCTYPE html>**:
   - Declares the document as HTML5 to the browser.
   - Ensures proper rendering of the page.

2. **<html>**:
   - The root element that contains all other HTML elements.
   - The lang attribute specifies the language of the document (e.g., en for English).

3. **<head>**:
   - Contains metadata about the document (e.g., character encoding, title, and linked stylesheets).

4. **<meta>**:
   - **charset="UTF-8"**:
     - Defines character encoding to ensure special characters display correctly.
   - **viewport**:
     - Ensures responsive behavior on mobile devices.

5. **<title>**:
   - Sets the title displayed on the browser tab.

6. **<body>**:

    o   Contains the visible content of the web page.

**Common HTML Elements**

HTML elements are the building blocks of web pages. They define headings, text, links, images, and more.

*1. Headings*

Headings structure the content hierarchy of a page. They range from <h1> (most important) to <h6> (least important).

**Example**:

html
Copy code

```
<h1>Main Heading</h1>
<h2>Subheading</h2>
<h3>Sub-subheading</h3>
```

*2. Paragraphs*

Paragraphs are used for blocks of text.

**Example**:

html
Copy code

<p>This is a paragraph of text. It can span multiple lines in the browser.</p>


### 3. Links

Links connect users to other web pages or resources.

**Example**:

html

Copy code

```
<a href="https://example.com" target="_blank">Visit Example</a>
```

- **href**: Specifies the URL.
- **target="_blank"**: Opens the link in a new tab.


### 4. Images

Images enhance content visually.

**Example**:

html

Copy code

```
<img src="images/logo.png" alt="Website Logo">
```

- **src**: Specifies the image path.

- **alt**: Provides alternative text for accessibility.

## Semantic HTML

Semantic HTML introduces meaningful tags that describe the purpose of content, improving readability and SEO.

### 1. *<header>*

Defines the introductory content or navigation of a section or page.

**Example**:

html
Copy code

```
<header>
 <h1>My Blog</h1>
 <nav>
  <a href="index.html">Home</a>
  <a href="about.html">About</a>
 </nav>
</header>
```

### 2. *<footer>*

Defines the footer content, such as copyright or contact information.

**Example**:

html

Copy code

```
<footer>
  <p>&copy; 2024 My Blog. All rights reserved.</p>
</footer>
```

### 3. *<section>*

Groups related content into thematic sections.

**Example**:

html

Copy code

```
<section>
  <h2>Latest Articles</h2>
  <p>Read our most recent posts below.</p>
</section>
```

### 4. *<article>*

Represents standalone content, such as a blog post or news item.

**Example**:

html

Copy code

```
<article>
  <h3>How to Learn HTML5</h3>
  <p>HTML5 is the building block of the web...</p>
</article>
```

## Real-World Example: Creating the Structure for a Blog Homepage

Let's build a basic structure for a blog homepage using the concepts we've covered.

### *HTML Code:*

html

Copy code

```
<!DOCTYPE html>
<html lang="en">
<head>
  <meta charset="UTF-8">
  <meta name="viewport" content="width=device-width, initial-scale=1.0">
  <title>My Blog</title>
</head>
<body>
  <!-- Header -->
  <header>
```

```html
  <h1>Welcome to My Blog</h1>
  <nav>
    <a href="index.html">Home</a>
    <a href="about.html">About</a>
    <a href="contact.html">Contact</a>
  </nav>
</header>

<!-- Main Content -->
<main>
  <!-- Section for Latest Posts -->
  <section>
    <h2>Latest Articles</h2>

    <!-- First Article -->
    <article>
      <h3>How to Learn HTML5</h3>
      <p>HTML5 is a powerful language for structuring web pages...</p>
      <a href="article1.html">Read More</a>
    </article>

    <!-- Second Article -->
    <article>
      <h3>Understanding CSS3</h3>
```

```
<p>CSS3 is the design language that brings your web pages
to life...</p>
    <a href="article2.html">Read More</a>
  </article>
 </section>
</main>

<!-- Footer -->
<footer>
 <p>&copy; 2024 My Blog. All rights reserved.</p>
 </footer>
</body>
</html>
```

## Explanation:

1. **Header**:
   - o Contains the blog's title and navigation menu.

2. **Main Section**:
   - o A section groups articles with headings, summaries, and links.

3. **Footer**:
   - o Displays copyright information.

1. **HTML5 Structure**:

 o A clean document structure ensures compatibility and readability.

2. **Essential Elements**:

 o Headings, paragraphs, links, and images form the foundation of web content.

3. **Semantic Tags**:

 o Tags like <header>, <footer>, and <section> enhance accessibility and SEO.

4. **Practical Example**:

 o The blog homepage demonstrates how to combine elements and semantics into a functional layout.


In the next chapter, we'll explore the basics of **CSS3**, adding styles to transform this structured page into a visually engaging design. Let's get creative!

# CHAPTER 4: BASICS OF CSS3

CSS3 (Cascading Style Sheets, version 3) is the styling language of the web. While HTML5 provides the structure of a web page, CSS3 brings it to life with colors, layouts, fonts, and much more. In this chapter, we'll learn how to link a CSS file to an HTML document, understand CSS syntax, explore different ways to apply CSS, and apply these concepts to style the blog homepage created in the previous chapter.

**Linking a CSS File to an HTML Document**

To style an HTML document, CSS rules need to be linked or embedded into the page.

*1. Linking an External CSS File*

The preferred way to apply CSS is to use an external file. This keeps the HTML clean and makes styles reusable across multiple pages.

**Steps to Link a CSS File:**

1. Create a CSS file (e.g., styles.css) in the project's css/ folder.

2. Link the file in the <head> section of the HTML document using the <link> tag.

**Example**:

html

Copy code

```
<head>
  <link rel="stylesheet" href="css/styles.css">
</head>
```

## 2. Inline CSS

Inline styles are applied directly to individual HTML elements using the style attribute. This method is rarely used due to poor maintainability.

**Example**:

html

Copy code

```
<h1 style="color: blue; font-size: 24px;">Welcome to My Blog</h1>
```

## 3. Internal CSS

Internal styles are placed within a <style> tag in the <head> section of the HTML document. While useful for quick testing, internal CSS is not recommended for larger projects.

**Example**:

html
Copy code

```
<head>
  <style>
    h1 {
      color: blue;
      font-size: 24px;
    }
  </style>
</head>
```

**CSS Syntax: Selectors, Properties, and Values**

*1. CSS Selectors*

Selectors specify which HTML elements the styles will apply to.

**Common Selectors**:

- **Element Selector**: Targets all elements of a specific type (e.g., all <h1> tags).

```css
css
Copy code
h1 {
  color: blue;
}
```

- **Class Selector**: Targets elements with a specific class, denoted by a period (.).

```css
css
Copy code
.highlight {
  background-color: yellow;
}
```

HTML Example:

```html
html
Copy code
<p class="highlight">This text has a yellow background.</p>
```

- **ID Selector**: Targets a single element with a specific ID, denoted by a hash (#).

```css
css
Copy code
```

```
#main-title {
  font-size: 32px;
}
```

HTML Example:

html
Copy code
```
<h1 id="main-title">Main Title</h1>
```

## 2. CSS Properties and Values

CSS styles are applied using properties (e.g., color, font-size) and values.

**Example**:

css
Copy code
```
h1 {
  color: blue;       /* Sets the text color */
  font-size: 24px;   /* Sets the font size */
  text-align: center; /* Aligns the text to the center */
}
```

## Inline, Internal, and External CSS Styles

Let's compare these methods using an example:

**HTML**:

html

Copy code

```
<!DOCTYPE html>
<html lang="en">
<head>
  <meta charset="UTF-8">
  <meta name="viewport" content="width=device-width, initial-scale=1.0">
  <title>CSS Example</title>
  <link rel="stylesheet" href="css/styles.css"> <!-- External CSS -->
  <style>
   h1 { color: red; } <!-- Internal CSS -->
  </style>
</head>
<body>
  <h1 style="font-size: 32px;">Hello, World!</h1> <!-- Inline CSS -->
</body>
</html>
```

**Explanation**:

- **Inline CSS** overrides both internal and external CSS due to higher specificity.
- **Internal CSS** takes precedence over external CSS unless overridden by inline styles.

### Real-World Example: Styling the Blog Homepage

Using external CSS, we'll style the blog homepage created in Chapter 3.

***CSS File (css/styles.css):***

```css
css
Copy code
/* General Styles */
body {
  font-family: Arial, sans-serif;
  margin: 0;
  padding: 0;
  line-height: 1.6;
  background-color: #f4f4f4;
}

/* Header */
header {
  background-color: #007bff;
```

```css
  color: white;
  padding: 1em 0;
  text-align: center;
}

header h1 {
  margin: 0;
  font-size: 2.5em;
}

/* Navigation */
nav {
  margin-top: 10px;
}

nav a {
  color: white;
  text-decoration: none;
  margin: 0 10px;
}

nav a:hover {
  text-decoration: underline;
}
```

```css
/* Main Section */
main {
  padding: 20px;
}

section h2 {
  color: #333;
}

article {
  background: white;
  margin: 20px 0;
  padding: 15px;
  border-radius: 5px;
  box-shadow: 0 2px 5px rgba(0, 0, 0, 0.1);
}

article h3 {
  margin-top: 0;
}

article a {
  color: #007bff;
  text-decoration: none;
}
```

```css
article a:hover {
  text-decoration: underline;
}

/* Footer */
footer {
  background-color: #333;
  color: white;
  text-align: center;
  padding: 10px 0;
  position: relative;
  bottom: 0;
  width: 100%;
}
```

***HTML File (Updated) (index.html):***

html

Copy code

```html
<!DOCTYPE html>
<html lang="en">
<head>
  <meta charset="UTF-8">
  <meta name="viewport" content="width=device-width, initial-scale=1.0">
```

```
<title>My Blog</title>
<link rel="stylesheet" href="css/styles.css">
</head>
<body>
 <header>
  <h1>Welcome to My Blog</h1>
  <nav>
   <a href="index.html">Home</a>
   <a href="about.html">About</a>
   <a href="contact.html">Contact</a>
  </nav>
 </header>

 <main>
  <section>
   <h2>Latest Articles</h2>

   <article>
    <h3>How to Learn HTML5</h3>
    <p>HTML5 is a powerful language for structuring web
pages...</p>
    <a href="article1.html">Read More</a>
   </article>

   <article>
```

```html
<h3>Understanding CSS3</h3>
<p>CSS3 is the design language that brings your web pages
to life...</p>
<a href="article2.html">Read More</a>
</article>
</section>
</main>


<footer>
<p>&copy; 2024 My Blog. All rights reserved.</p>
</footer>
</body>
</html>
```

***Result:***

1. **Header**:
   - o A blue background with white text and a clean navigation menu.

2. **Main Section**:
   - o Articles are displayed in card-like blocks with shadows and rounded corners.

3. **Footer**:
   - o A fixed-width footer with a dark background and centered text.

**Key Takeaways**

1. **External CSS**:
   - o Recommended for large projects as it separates content and styling.
2. **CSS Syntax**:
   - o Selectors, properties, and values are the foundation of CSS.
3. **Flexibility**:
   - o Inline, internal, and external CSS styles offer different levels of control.
4. **Practical Application**:
   - o Styling transforms a simple HTML page into an engaging, user-friendly design.

In the next chapter, we'll explore the **box model**, a fundamental concept for creating layouts and understanding spacing in CSS. Let's dive deeper into the mechanics of CSS!

# CHAPTER 5: UNDERSTANDING THE BOX MODEL

The CSS box model is a foundational concept in web design, as it determines how elements are sized and spaced on a web page. This chapter explores the components of the box model, explains the differences between content-box and border-box, provides debugging tips for layout issues, and culminates with a real-world example of creating a simple card layout.

**Elements of the Box Model**

In the box model, every HTML element is treated as a rectangular box with four distinct areas:

1. **Content**:
   - The core area where text, images, or other content is displayed.
   - Defined by the width and height properties.
2. **Padding**:
   - The space between the content and the border.

o Adds internal spacing within the element.

3. **Border**:

   o Surrounds the padding and content.

   o Can be styled with different widths, colors, and patterns.

4. **Margin**:

   o The space between the element and its neighboring elements.

   o Does not include background or border styling.

## *Visualization of the Box Model*

diff

Copy code

```
+-------------------------+
|     Margin       |
+-------------------------+
|     Border        |
+-------------------------+
|     Padding       |
+-------------------------+
|     Content       |
+-------------------------+
```

## *Example CSS Styling of the Box Model*

css

Copy code

```
.card {
  width: 300px; /* Width of the content */
  padding: 20px; /* Space inside the card */
  border: 2px solid #ccc; /* Card border */
  margin: 10px; /* Space outside the card */
}
```

## Box-Sizing: content-box vs. border-box

The box-sizing property controls how the total size of an element is calculated.

### 1. Default Behavior: content-box

- The width and height apply only to the content area.
- Padding and border are **added** to the total size of the element.

**Example**:

css
Copy code
```
.card {
  width: 300px;
  padding: 20px;
  border: 2px solid #ccc;
}
```

**Result**:

- Content width = 300px.
- Total width = 300px (content) + 20px (padding) + 2px (border) = **344px**.

## 2. Modern Approach: border-box

- The width and height include padding and border.
- The content area shrinks to accommodate padding and border.

**Example**:

css
Copy code
```
.card {
  box-sizing: border-box;
  width: 300px;
  padding: 20px;
  border: 2px solid #ccc;
}
```
**Result**:

- Total width = 300px (no extra calculation).
- Content width = 300px - 20px (padding) - 2px (border) = **278px**.

### *Setting a Global border-box*

To simplify layouts, apply box-sizing: border-box globally:

css

Copy code

```
* {
  box-sizing: border-box;
}
```

### Debugging Layout Issues with Developer Tools

Browser developer tools provide insights into how the box model is applied to elements.

### *Steps to Inspect the Box Model:*

1. Open your website in a browser.
2. Right-click an element and select **Inspect**.
3. In the **Elements** panel, select an element to view its box model.
4. The box model section highlights:
   - Content, padding, border, and margin dimensions.
   - Total size of the element.

### *Common Layout Issues:*

1. **Unexpected Element Size**:
   - o Issue: Total size is larger than expected due to content-box.
   - o Solution: Switch to border-box for consistent sizing.

2. **Overlapping Margins**:
   - o Issue: Adjacent elements' vertical margins collapse into one.
   - o Solution: Add padding or use margin: 0 to prevent collapsing.

3. **Misaligned Elements**:
   - o Issue: Uneven spacing caused by inconsistent margins or padding.
   - o Solution: Use developer tools to measure spacing and adjust CSS.

**Real-World Example: Building a Simple Card Layout**

Let's create a card layout using the box model.

*HTML:*

html

Copy code

```
<!DOCTYPE html>
<html lang="en">
<head>
```

```html
  <meta charset="UTF-8">
  <meta name="viewport" content="width=device-width, initial-scale=1.0">
  <title>Card Layout</title>
  <link rel="stylesheet" href="styles.css">
</head>
<body>
  <div class="card">
    <h3>Card Title</h3>
    <p>This is a simple card layout. It uses the CSS box model for spacing and styling.</p>
    <a href="#" class="btn">Learn More</a>
  </div>
</body>
</html>
```

***CSS (styles.css):***

css

Copy code

```css
/* Global Settings */
* {
  box-sizing: border-box;
  margin: 0;
  padding: 0;
}
```

```css
body {
  font-family: Arial, sans-serif;
  background-color: #f4f4f4;
  padding: 20px;
  display: flex;
  justify-content: center;
  align-items: center;
  height: 100vh;
}

/* Card Styling */
.card {
  width: 300px;
  padding: 20px;
  border: 1px solid #ccc;
  border-radius: 8px; /* Rounded corners */
  background-color: white;
  box-shadow: 0 4px 6px rgba(0, 0, 0, 0.1); /* Shadow effect */
  text-align: center;
}

.card h3 {
  margin-bottom: 15px;
  color: #333;
```

```css
}

.card p {
  margin-bottom: 20px;
  color: #666;
}

.card .btn {
  display: inline-block;
  padding: 10px 20px;
  background-color: #007bff;
  color: white;
  text-decoration: none;
  border-radius: 5px;
  transition: background-color 0.3s;
}

.card .btn:hover {
  background-color: #0056b3;
}
```

*Result:*

1. **Appearance**:
   - A centered card with a shadow and rounded corners.

o Includes a title, description, and a call-to-action button.

2. **Box Model in Action**:

   o The padding creates internal spacing within the card.

   o The margin centers the card within the viewport.

   o The border and box-shadow define the card's edges and depth.

1. **Box Model Basics**:

   o Content, padding, border, and margin collectively determine the size and position of an element.

2. **Box-Sizing**:

   o Use border-box globally for simpler size calculations.

3. **Debugging**:

   o Developer tools provide a visual breakdown of the box model for any element.

4. **Practical Application**:

   o The card layout demonstrates how the box model influences real-world designs.

In the next chapter, we'll explore **Flexbox**, a powerful CSS layout tool that simplifies aligning and distributing elements in a responsive manner. Let's dive into modern layout techniques!

# CHAPTER 6: INTRODUCTION TO FLEXBOX

Flexbox (Flexible Box Layout) is a modern CSS layout module that provides powerful tools to align, distribute, and size elements within a container—even when their sizes are dynamic or unknown. Flexbox simplifies creating responsive designs, making it an essential tool for building layouts that work seamlessly across devices.

**What is Flexbox, and Why is It Essential for Responsive Design?**

*What is Flexbox?*
Flexbox is a one-dimensional layout model designed to arrange items in a row (horizontal) or column (vertical). Unlike traditional layout techniques (e.g., floats or inline-block), Flexbox

automatically adjusts elements' sizes and spacing based on the available space.

### *Why is Flexbox Essential for Responsive Design?*

1. **Flexibility**:
   o Automatically adjusts the size and position of items based on the container's dimensions.
2. **Simplified Alignment**:
   o Easily aligns items vertically and horizontally without extra CSS rules.
3. **Dynamic Sizing**:
   o Ensures elements maintain proportional sizes, even when content changes.
4. **Reordering**:
   o Allows you to change the visual order of elements without altering the HTML structure.

### Flex Container Properties

A Flexbox layout begins with a **flex container**. The container applies flex properties to its child elements (flex items).

### *1. display: flex*
To enable Flexbox, set the display property of the parent container to flex:

css

```
Copy code
.container {
  display: flex;
}
```

## 2. flex-direction

Defines the main axis along which items are placed in the container.

- **row** (default): Items are arranged horizontally, left to right.
- **row-reverse**: Items are arranged horizontally, right to left.
- **column**: Items are arranged vertically, top to bottom.
- **column-reverse**: Items are arranged vertically, bottom to top.

**Example**:

```
css
Copy code
.container {
  display: flex;
  flex-direction: row;
}
```

## 3. justify-content

Controls how items are distributed along the main axis.

- **flex-start** (default): Items align at the start of the axis.
- **flex-end**: Items align at the end of the axis.
- **center**: Items align at the center of the axis.
- **space-between**: Items are evenly distributed, with space between them.
- **space-around**: Items are evenly distributed, with space around them.
- **space-evenly**: Items are evenly distributed, with equal space between and around them.

**Example**:

css
Copy code
```
.container {
  display: flex;
  justify-content: space-between;
}
```

## 4. align-items

Controls how items align along the cross axis (perpendicular to the main axis).

- **stretch** (default): Items stretch to fill the container (if not constrained).
- **flex-start**: Items align at the start of the cross axis.
- **flex-end**: Items align at the end of the cross axis.
- **center**: Items align at the center of the cross axis.
- **baseline**: Items align based on their text baselines.

**Example**:

css
Copy code
.container {
  display: flex;
  align-items: center;
}

**Flex Item Properties**

Flex items (children of a flex container) can have individual properties to control their size and position.

*1. flex-grow*

Specifies how much an item should grow relative to others when extra space is available.

- **0** (default): Item does not grow.
- **1**: Item grows proportionally to available space.

**Example**:

css
Copy code
```
.item {
  flex-grow: 1; /* Item grows to fill available space */
}
```

## 2. flex-shrink

Specifies how much an item should shrink relative to others when space is limited.

- **0**: Item does not shrink.
- **1** (default): Item shrinks proportionally.

**Example**:

css
Copy code
```
.item {
  flex-shrink: 0; /* Item won't shrink when space is limited */
}
```

## 3. order

Defines the order in which items appear in the container, overriding the HTML order.

- **Default value**: 0.
- Higher values appear later, lower values appear earlier.

**Example**:

css

Copy code

```
.item:nth-child(2) {
  order: -1; /* Moves the second item to the first position */
}
```

## Real-World Example: Creating a Responsive Navigation Bar with Flexbox

Let's use Flexbox to create a navigation bar that adjusts its layout based on screen size.

### *HTML:*

html

Copy code

```
<!DOCTYPE html>
<html lang="en">
<head>
  <meta charset="UTF-8">
```

```html
    <meta name="viewport" content="width=device-width, initial-scale=1.0">
    <title>Responsive Navigation Bar</title>
    <link rel="stylesheet" href="styles.css">
</head>
<body>
  <header>
    <div class="logo">MyLogo</div>
    <nav>
      <ul class="nav-links">
        <li><a href="#home">Home</a></li>
        <li><a href="#about">About</a></li>
        <li><a href="#services">Services</a></li>
        <li><a href="#contact">Contact</a></li>
      </ul>
    </nav>
  </header>
</body>
</html>
```

**CSS (styles.css):**

css

Copy code

```css
/* General Reset */
* {
```

```css
  margin: 0;
  padding: 0;
  box-sizing: border-box;
}

body {
  font-family: Arial, sans-serif;
}

/* Header */
header {
  display: flex;
  justify-content: space-between; /* Space between logo and navigation */
  align-items: center; /* Center items vertically */
  padding: 10px 20px;
  background-color: #007bff;
  color: white;
}

/* Logo */
.logo {
  font-size: 1.5em;
  font-weight: bold;
}
```

```css
/* Navigation */
nav {
  flex-grow: 1; /* Take remaining space */
}

.nav-links {
  display: flex;
  justify-content: flex-end; /* Align links to the right */
  list-style: none;
}

.nav-links li {
  margin: 0 10px;
}

.nav-links a {
  text-decoration: none;
  color: white;
  font-weight: bold;
}

.nav-links a:hover {
  text-decoration: underline;
}
```

*Result:*

1. **Navigation Bar Layout**:
   o The logo is aligned to the left.
   o The navigation links are aligned to the right.
   o Links are evenly spaced, and hover effects are applied.

2. **Responsive Behavior**:
   o Add media queries to adjust the navigation for smaller screens (e.g., collapsing links into a dropdown menu).

1. **Flexbox Basics**:
   o Use display: flex to create flexible layouts.

2. **Container Properties**:
   o justify-content and align-items control item alignment.
   o flex-direction determines the layout axis.

3. **Item Properties**:
   o flex-grow, flex-shrink, and order customize item behavior.

4. **Practical Application**:

- o  Flexbox simplifies building responsive components, like navigation bars.

In the next chapter, we'll dive into **CSS Grid**, a powerful tool for two-dimensional layouts, and compare it with Flexbox. Let's elevate your layout skills!

# CHAPTER 7: GRID LAYOUT BASICS

CSS Grid Layout is a powerful, two-dimensional system for creating complex and responsive web layouts. Unlike Flexbox, which excels at handling one-dimensional layouts (rows or columns), Grid is designed to manage both rows and columns simultaneously. In this chapter, we'll explore the key concepts of CSS Grid, learn the differences between Grid and Flexbox, and build a responsive photo gallery as a real-world example.

**Difference Between Flexbox and CSS Grid**

*Flexbox: One-Dimensional Layout*

- Focuses on arranging items in a single row or column.
- Best for components like navigation bars or lists.

### CSS Grid: Two-Dimensional Layout

- Handles both rows and columns.
- Ideal for complex layouts like dashboards or galleries.

**Key Comparison**:

| Feature | Flexbox | CSS Grid |
|---|---|---|
| Layout Dimension | One-dimensional (row/column) | Two-dimensional (row+column) |
| Content Alignment | Content-driven | Layout-driven |
| Use Cases | Navigation bars, buttons | Page layouts, photo galleries |

### Grid Container and Item Properties

To use Grid, start by defining a **grid container** with display: grid. This container divides its space into a grid of rows and columns, where child elements (grid items) can be placed.

### 1. grid-template-columns

Defines the number and size of columns in the grid.

**Example**:

css

Copy code

```
.container {
  display: grid;
  grid-template-columns: 1fr 1fr 1fr; /* Three equal-width columns */
}
```

- fr (fractional unit): Allocates a fraction of the available space.
- Fixed widths like px, em, or % can also be used.

## 2. grid-template-rows

Defines the number and size of rows in the grid.

**Example**:

css

Copy code

```
.container {
  display: grid;
  grid-template-rows: 100px auto; /* One fixed row and one flexible row */
}
```

## 3. gap

Adds spacing between rows and columns.

**Example**:

css
Copy code

```
.container {
  display: grid;
  grid-template-columns: 1fr 1fr;
  gap: 20px; /* Adds 20px between rows and columns */
}
```

### 4. grid-area

Assigns a grid item to a specific area within the grid. Use with grid-template-areas in the container.

**Example**:

css
Copy code

```
.container {
  display: grid;
  grid-template-areas:
    "header header"
    "sidebar main";
}
```

```css
.header {
  grid-area: header;
}

.sidebar {
  grid-area: sidebar;
}

.main {
  grid-area: main;
}
```

## Explicit and Implicit Grids

### 1. Explicit Grids

Defined explicitly using grid-template-rows and grid-template-columns.

**Example**:

css
Copy code

```css
.container {
  display: grid;
  grid-template-columns: 200px 1fr; /* Explicitly defines two columns */
}
```

```
}
```

## 2. Implicit Grids

Automatically generated when items exceed the explicitly defined rows or columns.

**Example**:

```
css
Copy code
.container {
  display: grid;
  grid-template-columns: 200px;
}


.item {
  grid-column: span 2; /* Spans two columns, generating new rows
as needed */
}
```

## Real-World Example: Designing a Responsive Photo Gallery

Let's build a responsive photo gallery using CSS Grid.

*HTML:*

```
html
```

Copy code

```html
<!DOCTYPE html>
<html lang="en">
<head>
  <meta charset="UTF-8">
  <meta name="viewport" content="width=device-width, initial-scale=1.0">
  <title>Photo Gallery</title>
  <link rel="stylesheet" href="styles.css">
</head>
<body>
  <header>
    <h1>Photo Gallery</h1>
  </header>
  <main class="gallery">
    <img src="photo1.jpg" alt="Photo 1">
    <img src="photo2.jpg" alt="Photo 2">
    <img src="photo3.jpg" alt="Photo 3">
    <img src="photo4.jpg" alt="Photo 4">
    <img src="photo5.jpg" alt="Photo 5">
    <img src="photo6.jpg" alt="Photo 6">
  </main>
</body>
</html>
```

### *CSS (styles.css):*

css

Copy code

```css
/* General Styles */
body {
  font-family: Arial, sans-serif;
  margin: 0;
  padding: 0;
  text-align: center;
  background-color: #f4f4f4;
}

header {
  padding: 20px;
  background-color: #007bff;
  color: white;
}

h1 {
  margin: 0;
}

/* Grid Styles for Gallery */
.gallery {
  display: grid;
```

```css
grid-template-columns: repeat(auto-fit, minmax(150px, 1fr)); /*
Responsive columns */
  gap: 10px;
  padding: 20px;
}

.gallery img {
  width: 100%;
  border-radius: 8px;
  box-shadow: 0 4px 6px rgba(0, 0, 0, 0.1);
  transition: transform 0.2s;
}

.gallery img:hover {
  transform: scale(1.05); /* Slight zoom on hover */
}
```

*Explanation:*

1. **Responsive Columns**:
   o repeat(auto-fit, minmax(150px, 1fr)): Dynamically creates columns based on the screen size, ensuring each image is at least 150px wide.
2. **Spacing**:
   o gap: 10px: Adds spacing between the images.

3. **Hover Effect**:
   - transform: scale(1.05): Creates a subtle zoom effect when an image is hovered.

*Result:*

- **Desktop**: Images are displayed in multiple columns.
- **Tablet**: Columns adjust to fit fewer images per row.
- **Mobile**: Images stack into a single column for smaller screens.

1. **Grid Layout Advantages**:
   - Handles complex layouts with ease by managing rows and columns simultaneously.
2. **Key Properties**:
   - grid-template-columns, gap, and grid-area provide control over the layout.
3. **Explicit vs. Implicit Grids**:
   - Explicit grids define structure, while implicit grids handle overflow dynamically.
4. **Real-World Use Case**:
   - The responsive photo gallery demonstrates the flexibility of CSS Grid for layout design.

In the next chapter, we'll explore **Responsive Typography**, focusing on techniques to scale text effectively across different screen sizes. Let's continue building adaptable, user-friendly designs!

# CHAPTER 8: RESPONSIVE TYPOGRAPHY

Typography plays a critical role in web design, as it ensures that content is readable, engaging, and accessible. Responsive typography dynamically adjusts text sizes, line heights, and spacing to accommodate different screen sizes and resolutions. This chapter explores the use of relative units, setting a scalable base font size, scaling typography with media queries, and creating a real-world typography scale for a landing page.

## Using Relative Units: em, rem, and %

Relative units allow text to scale proportionally, ensuring consistency across devices and screen sizes. Unlike absolute units (e.g., px), relative units adapt to the parent or root element.

### 1. em (Relative to Parent)

- The size of 1em is equal to the computed font size of the parent element.
- Useful for nested elements.

**Example**:

css

Copy code

```
body {
  font-size: 16px; /* Base font size */
}


h1 {
  font-size: 2em; /* 2 × 16px = 32px */
}
```

## 2. rem (Relative to Root Element)

- The size of 1rem is based on the font size of the root element (<html>), making it predictable and consistent.

**Example**:

css

Copy code

```
html {
  font-size: 16px; /* Base font size */
```

```
}
```

```
p {
  font-size: 1.25rem; /* 1.25 × 16px = 20px */
}
```

### 3. % (Relative to Parent)

- Sets font size as a percentage of the parent's size.
- Less common than em or rem.

**Example**:

css
Copy code
```
body {
  font-size: 100%; /* 100% of browser's default size (usually 16px) */
}
```

```
p {
  font-size: 125%; /* 125% of 16px = 20px */
}
```

**Setting a Base Font Size for Scalability**

## *Best Practices for Setting a Base Font Size*

1. **Default Size**:
   o The browser's default size is typically 16px.
   o Set the base font size in the <html> element.

**Example**:

css

Copy code

```
html {
  font-size: 16px; /* Default size for desktop screens */
}
```

2. **Mobile-First Approach**:
   o Use a smaller base size for mobile devices and scale up for larger screens.

**Example**:

css

Copy code

```
html {
  font-size: 14px; /* Smaller size for mobile */
}

@media (min-width: 768px) {
  html {
```

```
    font-size: 16px; /* Larger size for tablets and desktops */
  }
}
```

### *Advantages of Using rem as a Base*

- Simplifies scaling across the entire website.
- Changes in the root font size automatically propagate to all rem-based elements.

### Techniques for Scaling Typography with Media Queries

Media queries allow text to adjust dynamically based on the viewport size.

### *1. Adjust Font Sizes*

Increase or decrease font sizes based on screen width.

### **Example**:

css

Copy code

```
html {
  font-size: 14px;
}


@media (min-width: 768px) {
```

```css
html {
  font-size: 16px;
  }
}
```

```css
@media (min-width: 1200px) {
 html {
  font-size: 18px;
  }
}
```

## 2. Scale Headings Proportionally

Use media queries to define larger heading sizes for bigger screens.

**Example**:

css
Copy code

```css
h1 {
  font-size: 2rem; /* Default for mobile */
}
```

```css
@media (min-width: 768px) {
 h1 {
  font-size: 2.5rem;
  }
}
```

```
}

@media (min-width: 1200px) {
  h1 {
    font-size: 3rem;
  }
}
```

### 3. Line Height and Spacing

Maintain readability by adjusting line height and letter spacing.

**Example**:

css
Copy code
```
p {
  font-size: 1rem;
  line-height: 1.6; /* 160% of font size */
  letter-spacing: 0.02em; /* Slightly spaced letters */
}
```

**Real-World Example: Designing a Typography Scale for a Landing Page**

*Goal*

Create a responsive typography system for a landing page that adapts gracefully to different screen sizes.

### HTML:

html

Copy code

```
<!DOCTYPE html>
<html lang="en">
<head>
  <meta charset="UTF-8">
  <meta name="viewport" content="width=device-width, initial-scale=1.0">
  <title>Responsive Typography</title>
  <link rel="stylesheet" href="styles.css">
</head>
<body>
  <header>
    <h1>Welcome to Our Website</h1>
    <p>Your journey starts here. Let's make it memorable.</p>
  </header>
  <main>
    <section>
      <h2>Our Features</h2>
```

```
<p>Discover what makes us unique and why our platform is
perfect for your needs.</p>
   </section>
  </main>
</body>
</html>
```

**CSS (styles.css):**

```css
css
Copy code
/* Base Styles */
html {
  font-size: 14px; /* Mobile-first base size */
}

@media (min-width: 768px) {
  html {
    font-size: 16px; /* Larger size for tablets */
  }
}

@media (min-width: 1200px) {
  html {
    font-size: 18px; /* Largest size for desktops */
  }
}
```

```css
body {
  font-family: 'Arial', sans-serif;
  line-height: 1.6;
  color: #333;
  margin: 0;
  padding: 0;
  background-color: #f4f4f4;
  text-align: center;
}

/* Header Styles */
header {
  padding: 20px;
  background-color: #007bff;
  color: white;
}

header h1 {
  font-size: 2.5rem; /* Scales with viewport */
  margin-bottom: 10px;
}

header p {
  font-size: 1.25rem;
}
```

```
/* Section Styles */
section {
  padding: 20px;
}

section h2 {
  font-size: 2rem;
  margin-bottom: 10px;
}

section p {
  font-size: 1rem;
  margin-bottom: 20px;
}
```

***Result:***

1. **Mobile Devices**:
   - Base font size is smaller (14px) for compact content.
   - Headings and paragraphs are proportionally scaled for readability.
2. **Tablets**:
   - Font size increases to 16px, ensuring text remains readable on larger screens.

3. **Desktops**:

   o Font size further increases to 18px, emphasizing the spacious layout.

1. **Relative Units**:

   o Use rem for scalable typography, ensuring consistency across devices.

2. **Base Font Size**:

   o Establish a root font size to simplify scaling.

3. **Media Queries**:

   o Adjust font sizes and spacing for different screen widths to enhance readability.

4. **Practical Example**:

   o The landing page typography scale showcases responsive techniques in action.

In the next chapter, we'll explore **Media Queries**, the backbone of responsive design, and learn how to adapt layouts, typography, and images for various screen sizes. Let's continue refining your responsive design skills!

# CHAPTER 9: MEDIA QUERIES: THE BACKBONE OF RESPONSIVE DESIGN

Media queries are the foundation of responsive web design. They enable styles to adapt based on the device's screen size, resolution, orientation, and other features. In this chapter, we'll explore the syntax and usage of media queries, learn how to select appropriate breakpoints, apply conditional styles for different screen sizes, and create a responsive layout for mobile, tablet, and desktop views.

## Syntax and Usage of Media Queries

Media queries are conditional CSS rules that apply styles when certain conditions are met, such as a minimum screen width or device orientation.

### *Basic Syntax*

css

Copy code

```
@media (condition) {
  /* CSS rules */
}
```

**Example**:

css

Copy code

```
/* Default styles */
body {
  font-size: 16px;
}


/* Apply larger font size for screens wider than 768px */
@media (min-width: 768px) {
  body {
    font-size: 18px;
  }
}
```

### *Common Media Query Features*

    1.  **min-width**:

- Applies styles when the screen width is **greater than or equal to** the specified value.
- **Example**:

css
Copy code
```
@media (min-width: 768px) {
  body {
    background-color: lightblue;
  }
}
```

2. **max-width**:

- Applies styles when the screen width is **less than or equal to** the specified value.
- **Example**:

css
Copy code
```
@media (max-width: 480px) {
  body {
    font-size: 14px;
  }
}
```

3. **orientation**:

- o Targets devices in either **portrait** or **landscape** mode.
- o **Example**:

css

Copy code

```
@media (orientation: landscape) {
  body {
    background-color: lightgreen;
  }
}
```

4. **Combining Conditions**:

- o Use logical operators like and, or, and not to combine conditions.
- o **Example**:

css

Copy code

```
@media (min-width: 768px) and (orientation:
landscape) {
  body {
    background-color: lightcoral;
  }
}
```

## Breakpoints: Choosing the Right Ones for Your Design

Breakpoints are screen widths where your layout changes to fit different devices. While there's no universal rule for breakpoints, they should be chosen based on the content and design of your site.

### *Common Breakpoints:*

- **Mobile**: 0px–480px
- **Tablet**: 481px–768px
- **Small Desktop**: 769px–1024px
- **Large Desktop**: 1025px+

### *Custom Breakpoints:*

Analyze your content to determine where it needs to adapt. Test across devices and screen sizes to identify natural breakpoints.

### Example:

css
Copy code

```css
/* Mobile-first approach */
body {
  font-size: 14px;
}

@media (min-width: 768px) {
  body {
```

```css
    font-size: 16px; /* Tablet and larger screens */
  }
}
```

```css
@media (min-width: 1024px) {
  body {
    font-size: 18px; /* Desktop screens */
  }
}
```

## Applying Conditional Styles for Different Screen Sizes

Media queries allow you to apply specific styles based on screen size and other conditions. Here are some examples:

### 1. Changing Layouts

Switch between stacked and grid layouts.

css
Copy code
```css
/* Mobile: Stacked layout */
.container {
  display: flex;
  flex-direction: column;
}
```

```css
/* Tablet: Two-column layout */
```

```css
@media (min-width: 768px) {
  .container {
    flex-direction: row;
    flex-wrap: wrap;
  }
}
```

## 2. Adjusting Typography

Scale text sizes for readability on larger screens.

css

Copy code

```css
h1 {
  font-size: 2rem;
}

@media (min-width: 768px) {
  h1 {
    font-size: 2.5rem;
  }
}

@media (min-width: 1024px) {
  h1 {
    font-size: 3rem;
```

```
}
}
```

### 3. Hiding and Showing Elements

Show or hide navigation menus based on screen size.

css

Copy code

```
/* Mobile: Hide navigation menu */
.nav {
  display: none;
}


/* Tablet and larger: Show navigation menu */
@media (min-width: 768px) {
  .nav {
    display: block;
  }
}
```

## Real-World Example: Adapting a Layout for Mobile, Tablet, and Desktop Views

*Goal*

Create a responsive layout for a simple webpage with a header, main content, and a sidebar.

*HTML:*

html

Copy code

```
<!DOCTYPE html>
<html lang="en">
<head>
  <meta charset="UTF-8">
  <meta name="viewport" content="width=device-width, initial-scale=1.0">
  <title>Responsive Layout</title>
  <link rel="stylesheet" href="styles.css">
</head>
<body>
  <header class="header">
   <h1>My Responsive Site</h1>
  </header>
  <main class="main">
   <section class="content">
    <h2>Main Content</h2>
    <p>This is the main content of the page.</p>
   </section>
```

```html
    <aside class="sidebar">
      <h2>Sidebar</h2>
      <p>This is the sidebar content.</p>
    </aside>
  </main>
</body>
</html>
```

*CSS (styles.css):*

```css
css
Copy code
/* General Reset */
* {
  margin: 0;
  padding: 0;
  box-sizing: border-box;
}

body {
  font-family: Arial, sans-serif;
  line-height: 1.6;
  background-color: #f4f4f4;
}

/* Header Styles */
```

```css
.header {
  background-color: #007bff;
  color: white;
  padding: 20px;
  text-align: center;
}

/* Main Content Styles */
.main {
  display: flex;
  flex-direction: column; /* Mobile-first: stacked layout */
  padding: 20px;
}

.content {
  background: white;
  padding: 20px;
  margin-bottom: 20px;
  border-radius: 5px;
}

.sidebar {
  background: #eaeaea;
  padding: 20px;
  border-radius: 5px;
```

```css
}

/* Tablet View */
@media (min-width: 768px) {
  .main {
   flex-direction: row; /* Side-by-side layout */
  }

  .content {
   flex: 2; /* Takes up more space */
   margin-right: 20px;
  }

  .sidebar {
   flex: 1; /* Takes up less space */
  }
}

/* Desktop View */
@media (min-width: 1024px) {
  .main {
   padding: 40px;
  }

  .content, .sidebar {
```

```
    border-radius: 10px;

  }

}
```

*Result:*

1. **Mobile View**:
   o   The header spans the full width.
   o   The main content and sidebar are stacked vertically.
2. **Tablet View**:
   o   The main content and sidebar are displayed side-by-side, with the content section taking up more space.
3. **Desktop View**:
   o   Padding and border radii are enhanced for a more refined appearance.

1. **Media Query Syntax**:
   o   Use min-width, max-width, and logical operators to define conditional styles.
2. **Choosing Breakpoints**:
   o   Select breakpoints based on content and design, focusing on where the layout needs to adapt.
3. **Versatility**:

- o Media queries allow changes in layout, typography, visibility, and more.
4. **Practical Example**:
   - o The responsive layout demonstrates how to adapt a design for mobile, tablet, and desktop screens.

In the next chapter, we'll explore **Building a Mobile-First Layout**, where we'll focus on creating designs that scale up from smaller screens, ensuring efficient, adaptable web pages. Let's continue building responsive expertise!

# CHAPTER 10: BUILDING A MOBILE-FIRST LAYOUT

Mobile-first design prioritizes smaller screens, focusing on essential content and functionality before scaling up for larger devices. This approach ensures better usability on mobile devices and avoids bloated designs that don't translate well to smaller viewports. In this chapter, we'll explore the philosophy of mobile-first design, learn how to start with small screens and scale up, utilize CSS resets for consistency, and convert a desktop-centric design into a mobile-first layout.

**Philosophy of Mobile-First Design**

## *What is Mobile-First Design?*

Mobile-first design is a strategy where the layout and functionality are optimized for mobile devices first, then enhanced for larger screens using progressive enhancement.

## *Why Mobile-First?*

1. **Mobile Dominance**:
   o Mobile devices account for more than half of global web traffic.
2. **Performance Focus**:
   o Designing for mobile emphasizes speed and simplicity, avoiding unnecessary elements.
3. **Content Prioritization**:
   o Forces designers to focus on essential content and functionality.
4. **Future-Proofing**:
   o Mobile-first designs are better equipped to adapt to evolving device trends.

## *Principles of Mobile-First Design:*

- Start with a minimal design.
- Use progressive enhancement to add features for larger devices.
- Focus on touch-friendly navigation and interactions.

**Starting with the Smallest Screen and Scaling Up**

The mobile-first approach begins with base styles designed for small screens. Media queries are then used to add enhancements for larger screens.

### 1. Mobile-First Base Styles

Define styles for the smallest viewport (e.g., smartphones).

**Example**:

css
Copy code

```
body {
  font-family: Arial, sans-serif;
  font-size: 14px;
  margin: 0;
  padding: 0;
}

.header {
  text-align: center;
  padding: 10px;
  background-color: #007bff;
  color: white;
}
```

## 2. Scaling Up with Media Queries

Enhance the design for tablets and desktops using min-width media queries.

**Example**:

css

Copy code

```css
/* Tablet View */
@media (min-width: 768px) {
  .header {
    text-align: left;
    padding: 20px;
  }
}


/* Desktop View */
@media (min-width: 1024px) {
  body {
    font-size: 16px;
  }
}
```

## Using CSS Resets and Normalization for Consistency

Browsers apply default styles to HTML elements, which can vary between browsers. CSS resets and normalization ensure a consistent baseline across all browsers.

### 1. CSS Reset

A CSS reset removes all default browser styles.

**Example**:

css
Copy code
```
/* Simple CSS Reset */
* {
  margin: 0;
  padding: 0;
  box-sizing: border-box;
}
```

### 2. CSS Normalize

Normalization maintains useful browser defaults while providing consistency.

**Example**:

css
Copy code
```
/* Normalize CSS Example */
```

```css
html {
  font-size: 100%;
  line-height: 1.15;
}

body {
  margin: 0;
}
```

## Real-World Example: Converting a Desktop-Centric Design to Mobile-First

### Scenario

A website designed for desktops needs to be converted into a mobile-first layout. The layout includes a header, a main content area with two sections, and a footer.

### Desktop-Centric Design (Initial State)
**HTML**:

```html
html
Copy code
<!DOCTYPE html>
<html lang="en">
<head>
```

```html
  <meta charset="UTF-8">
  <meta name="viewport" content="width=device-width, initial-scale=1.0">
  <title>Desktop Design</title>
  <link rel="stylesheet" href="styles.css">
</head>
<body>
  <header class="header">
    <h1>Welcome to My Website</h1>
  </header>
  <main class="main">
    <section class="content">
      <h2>Main Content</h2>
      <p>This is the main content of the page.</p>
    </section>
    <aside class="sidebar">
      <h2>Sidebar</h2>
      <p>This is the sidebar content.</p>
    </aside>
  </main>
  <footer class="footer">
    <p>© 2024 My Website</p>
  </footer>
</body>
</html>
```

**Desktop-Centric CSS**:

css
Copy code

```css
/* Desktop Styles */
body {
  font-family: Arial, sans-serif;
  font-size: 16px;
}

.header {
  text-align: center;
  padding: 20px;
  background-color: #007bff;
  color: white;
}

.main {
  display: flex;
  justify-content: space-between;
  padding: 20px;
}

.content {
  flex: 2;
  margin-right: 20px;
```

```css
}

.sidebar {
  flex: 1;
}

.footer {
  text-align: center;
  padding: 10px;
  background-color: #333;
  color: white;
}
```

### *Mobile-First Conversion*
**Updated CSS**:

css
Copy code

```css
/* Base Mobile Styles */
body {
  font-family: Arial, sans-serif;
  font-size: 14px;
  margin: 0;
  padding: 0;
}
```

```css
.header {
  text-align: center;
  padding: 10px;
  background-color: #007bff;
  color: white;
}

.main {
  display: flex;
  flex-direction: column; /* Stacked layout for mobile */
  padding: 10px;
}

.content {
  margin-bottom: 20px; /* Adds spacing between sections */
}

.sidebar {
  background-color: #eaeaea;
  padding: 10px;
}

.footer {
  text-align: center;
```

```css
  padding: 10px;
  background-color: #333;
  color: white;
}


/* Tablet Styles */
@media (min-width: 768px) {
  .main {
    flex-direction: row; /* Side-by-side layout for tablet */
  }


  .content {
    margin-right: 20px;
    margin-bottom: 0;
  }
}


/* Desktop Styles */
@media (min-width: 1024px) {
  body {
    font-size: 16px;
  }


  .main {
    padding: 20px;
```

}

}

*Result*

1. **Mobile View**:
   - ○ Header, content, and sidebar are stacked vertically.
   - ○ Smaller font size and padding optimize the layout for small screens.
2. **Tablet View**:
   - ○ Content and sidebar are displayed side by side.
   - ○ Increased padding enhances the layout.
3. **Desktop View**:
   - ○ Font size and spacing are further increased for readability.

1. **Mobile-First Philosophy**:
   - ○ Start with essential styles for mobile devices and progressively enhance for larger screens.
2. **CSS Resets and Normalization**:
   - ○ Ensure a consistent baseline across browsers to simplify design.
3. **Practical Application**:

o The example demonstrates converting a desktop-centric layout to a responsive, mobile-first design.

4. **Scalability**:

o Using media queries ensures the design scales gracefully across devices.

In the next chapter, we'll explore **Working with Images in Responsive Design**, focusing on techniques to optimize and adapt images for different screen sizes while maintaining performance. Let's dive in!

# CHAPTER 11: WORKING WITH IMAGES IN RESPONSIVE DESIGN

Images are a vital part of web design, enhancing user experience and visual appeal. However, they can significantly impact page performance if not optimized. Responsive image techniques ensure images adapt to different screen sizes, resolutions, and network conditions. This chapter covers best practices for responsive images, the use of the <picture> element and srcset, lazy loading for performance improvement, and a practical example of building a responsive hero section.

## Best Practices for Responsive Images

1. **Use Optimized File Formats**:
   - **WebP**: Offers superior compression without loss of quality compared to JPEG and PNG.
   - **AVIF**: A newer format with even better compression than WebP.
   - **JPEG/PNG**: Still widely used but heavier compared to WebP/AVIF.

2. **Compress Images**:
   - Use tools like TinyPNG or ImageOptim to reduce file sizes.

3. **Choose Appropriate Dimensions**:
   - Resize images to match the largest size they'll be displayed.

4. **Leverage Responsive Techniques**:
   - Use CSS and HTML features like srcset, the <picture> element, and media queries.

5. **Optimize for Retina Displays**:
   - Provide higher-resolution images for devices with higher pixel densities (e.g., 2x or 3x).

6. **Test on Multiple Devices**:
   - Ensure images render correctly and maintain quality across different screen sizes and resolutions.

## Using the <picture> Element and srcset

### 1. <picture> Element

The <picture> element provides multiple sources for an image, allowing browsers to choose the most appropriate one based on media queries or formats.

**Example**:

html
Copy code
```
<picture>
  <source srcset="image-large.jpg" media="(min-width: 1024px)">
  <source srcset="image-medium.jpg" media="(min-width: 768px)">
  <img src="image-small.jpg" alt="Responsive example">
</picture>
```

- **<source>**: Defines alternative image sources with media queries.
- **Fallback <img>**: Used if none of the <source> conditions match.

### 2. srcset Attribute

The srcset attribute allows browsers to choose the best image resolution based on device pixel density.

**Example**:

html
Copy code

```
<img
  src="image-small.jpg"
  srcset="image-medium.jpg 2x, image-large.jpg 3x"
  alt="Responsive example">
```

- **2x or 3x**: Specifies images for higher-resolution displays.
- The browser automatically selects the appropriate image.

### Lazy Loading Images to Improve Performance

Lazy loading defers loading images until they're needed, such as when they appear in the viewport. This reduces initial page load time and bandwidth usage.

### 1. Using the loading Attribute

Modern browsers support the loading attribute to enable native lazy loading.

**Example**:

html

Copy code

```
<img src="image.jpg" alt="Lazy-loaded image" loading="lazy">
```

## 2. JavaScript Lazy Loading (Fallback for Older Browsers)

Use libraries like lazysizes for compatibility.

**Example**:

html

Copy code

```
<img class="lazyload" data-src="image.jpg" alt="Lazy-loaded image">
<script src="lazysizes.min.js" async></script>
```

## Real-World Example: Building a Responsive Hero Section

### Goal

Create a hero section with a responsive background image and lazy-loaded content.

### HTML:

html

Copy code

```
<!DOCTYPE html>
<html lang="en">
```

```
<head>
  <meta charset="UTF-8">
  <meta name="viewport" content="width=device-width, initial-scale=1.0">
  <title>Responsive Hero Section</title>
  <link rel="stylesheet" href="styles.css">
</head>
<body>
  <header class="hero">
    <picture>
      <source srcset="hero-large.jpg" media="(min-width: 1024px)">
      <source srcset="hero-medium.jpg" media="(min-width: 768px)">
      <img src="hero-small.jpg" alt="Hero background" class="hero-img">
    </picture>
    <div class="hero-content">
      <h1>Welcome to Our Website</h1>
      <p>Your journey begins here. Let us guide you.</p>
      <a href="#learn-more" class="btn">Learn More</a>
    </div>
  </header>
</body>
</html>
```

*CSS (styles.css):*

css

Copy code

```
/* General Reset */
* {
  margin: 0;
  padding: 0;
  box-sizing: border-box;
}

body {
  font-family: Arial, sans-serif;
  line-height: 1.6;
}

/* Hero Section */
.hero {
  position: relative;
  text-align: center;
  color: white;
  height: 100vh;
  display: flex;
  flex-direction: column;
  justify-content: center;
```

```css
    align-items: center;
    background-color: #000; /* Fallback background */
}

.hero-img {
    position: absolute;
    top: 0;
    left: 0;
    width: 100%;
    height: 100%;
    object-fit: cover; /* Ensures the image fills the container */
    z-index: -1;
}

.hero-content {
    z-index: 1; /* Ensures content appears above the background
image */
}

.hero h1 {
    font-size: 2.5rem;
    margin-bottom: 10px;
}

.hero p {
```

```css
  font-size: 1.2rem;
  margin-bottom: 20px;
}

.btn {
  display: inline-block;
  padding: 10px 20px;
  background-color: #007bff;
  color: white;
  text-decoration: none;
  border-radius: 5px;
  transition: background-color 0.3s;
}

.btn:hover {
  background-color: #0056b3;
}

/* Responsive Typography */
@media (min-width: 768px) {
  .hero h1 {
    font-size: 3rem;
  }

  .hero p {
```

```
    font-size: 1.5rem;

  }

}


@media (min-width: 1024px) {

  .hero h1 {

    font-size: 3.5rem;

  }


  .hero p {

    font-size: 1.75rem;

  }

}
```

### *Result*

1. **Mobile View**:
   - Displays a small, optimized background image with readable text.
2. **Tablet View**:
   - Loads a medium-sized image and increases text size.
3. **Desktop View**:
   - Uses the largest image and maximizes typography for a visually striking experience.

1. **Responsive Techniques**:
   - o Use the <picture> element and srcset to serve appropriately sized images.

2. **Performance Optimization**:
   - o Implement lazy loading to reduce initial load times and save bandwidth.

3. **Practical Application**:
   - o The hero section demonstrates how to combine responsive and performance-focused techniques.

4. **User Experience**:
   - o Ensuring images adapt to screen size and resolution enhances user engagement.

In the next chapter, we'll explore **Responsive Navigation Menus**, learning how to create mobile-friendly menus with dropdowns and hamburger icons. Let's continue refining your responsive design skills!

# CHAPTER 12: RESPONSIVE NAVIGATION MENUS

Navigation menus are crucial for user experience, providing access to a website's key sections. Responsive menus ensure usability across devices, from desktops to smartphones. This chapter explores techniques for creating mobile-friendly navigation, dropdown menus and hamburger icons with CSS, enhancing interactivity with JavaScript, and concludes with a real-world example of a responsive menu for a restaurant website.

**Techniques for Mobile-Friendly Navigation**

*1. Mobile-First Design*

- Design for the smallest screens first, then enhance for larger devices.
- Use stacked layouts for smaller viewports and horizontal layouts for desktops.

**Example**:

css
Copy code
```css
/* Mobile navigation (default) */
.nav {
  display: flex;
  flex-direction: column;
  align-items: flex-start;
}
```

*2. Flexbox for Alignment*

Flexbox simplifies aligning navigation links and creating dropdown menus.

**Example**:

css

Copy code

```
.nav {
  display: flex;
  justify-content: space-between;
}
```

### 3. Hide and Show Techniques

- Use CSS media queries to show/hide navigation elements based on screen size.
- Use JavaScript to toggle visibility dynamically.

**Example**:

css

Copy code

```
/* Hide navigation for mobile */
.nav {
  display: none;
}


/* Show navigation for larger screens */
@media (min-width: 768px) {
  .nav {
    display: flex;
  }
```

}

## Dropdown Menus and Hamburger Icons with CSS

### 1. Creating a Dropdown Menu

Use CSS to build simple dropdown menus that appear on hover.

**HTML**:

```html
<nav>
  <ul class="nav">
    <li><a href="#home">Home</a></li>
    <li class="dropdown">
      <a href="#menu">Menu</a>
      <ul class="dropdown-menu">
        <li><a href="#starters">Starters</a></li>
        <li><a href="#main-courses">Main Courses</a></li>
        <li><a href="#desserts">Desserts</a></li>
      </ul>
    </li>
    <li><a href="#contact">Contact</a></li>
  </ul>
</nav>
```

**CSS**:

css

Copy code

```css
/* General Navigation Styles */
.nav {
  list-style: none;
  display: flex;
  padding: 0;
}

.nav > li {
  position: relative;
  margin-right: 20px;
}

.nav a {
  text-decoration: none;
  padding: 10px;
  display: block;
}

/* Dropdown Menu */
.dropdown-menu {
  display: none; /* Hidden by default */
  position: absolute;
  top: 100%;
```

```css
    left: 0;
    background-color: white;
    border: 1px solid #ddd;
    list-style: none;
    padding: 0;
}

.dropdown-menu li {
    margin: 0;
}

.dropdown-menu a {
    padding: 10px 20px;
}

/* Show Dropdown on Hover */
.dropdown:hover .dropdown-menu {
    display: block;
}
```

## 2. Adding a Hamburger Icon

Use CSS to create a hamburger menu for mobile devices.

**HTML**:

html

Copy code

```
<button class="hamburger" aria-label="Toggle Navigation">
  <span></span>
  <span></span>
  <span></span>
</button>
<nav class="mobile-nav">
  <ul>
    <li><a href="#home">Home</a></li>
    <li><a href="#menu">Menu</a></li>
    <li><a href="#contact">Contact</a></li>
  </ul>
</nav>
```

**CSS**:

css

Copy code

```
/* Hamburger Icon */
.hamburger {
  display: flex;
  flex-direction: column;
  gap: 5px;
  width: 30px;
  background: none;
  border: none;
  cursor: pointer;
```

```css
}

.hamburger span {
  display: block;
  width: 100%;
  height: 4px;
  background-color: black;
}

/* Mobile Navigation Hidden by Default */
.mobile-nav {
  display: none;
}

@media (max-width: 768px) {
  .mobile-nav {
    display: block;
    list-style: none;
    padding: 0;
  }
}
```

## Enhancing Navigation with Basic JavaScript

### 1. Toggle Visibility

Use JavaScript to toggle the mobile navigation menu when the hamburger icon is clicked.

**JavaScript**:

javascript
Copy code

```
document.querySelector('.hamburger').addEventListener('click',  ()
=> {
  const mobileNav = document.querySelector('.mobile-nav');
  mobileNav.classList.toggle('open');
});
```

**CSS**:

css
Copy code

```css
/* Show Mobile Navigation When Open */
.mobile-nav.open {
  display: block;
}
```

**Real-World Example: Responsive Menu for a Restaurant Website**

*HTML:*

html
Copy code

```html
<!DOCTYPE html>
<html lang="en">
<head>
  <meta charset="UTF-8">
  <meta name="viewport" content="width=device-width, initial-scale=1.0">
  <title>Restaurant Menu</title>
  <link rel="stylesheet" href="styles.css">
</head>
<body>
  <header>
    <button class="hamburger" aria-label="Toggle Navigation">
      <span></span>
      <span></span>
      <span></span>
    </button>
    <nav>
      <ul class="nav">
        <li><a href="#home">Home</a></li>
        <li><a href="#about">About</a></li>
        <li><a href="#menu">Menu</a></li>
        <li><a href="#contact">Contact</a></li>
      </ul>
    </nav>
  </header>
```

```
</body>
</html>
```

***CSS (styles.css):***

```css
css
Copy code
/* Reset */
* {
  margin: 0;
  padding: 0;
  box-sizing: border-box;
}

body {
  font-family: Arial, sans-serif;
  line-height: 1.6;
}

header {
  display: flex;
  justify-content: space-between;
  align-items: center;
  padding: 10px 20px;
  background-color: #333;
  color: white;
```

```css
}

.nav {
  list-style: none;
  display: flex;
  gap: 20px;
}

.nav a {
  text-decoration: none;
  color: white;
}

/* Hamburger Menu */
.hamburger {
  display: none;
  flex-direction: column;
  gap: 5px;
  width: 30px;
  background: none;
  border: none;
  cursor: pointer;
}

.hamburger span {
```

```css
  display: block;
  width: 100%;
  height: 4px;
  background-color: white;
}

/* Mobile Navigation */
@media (max-width: 768px) {
 .nav {
   display: none;
 }

 .hamburger {
   display: flex;
 }

 .nav.open {
   display: flex;
   flex-direction: column;
   gap: 10px;
   margin-top: 10px;
 }
}
```

*JavaScript:*

javascript

Copy code

```
document.querySelector('.hamburger').addEventListener('click', ()
=> {
  const nav = document.querySelector('.nav');
  nav.classList.toggle('open');
});
```

**Result**

1. **Desktop View**:
   - The menu is displayed horizontally at the top of the page.
   - Dropdowns appear on hover.
2. **Mobile View**:
   - The hamburger menu toggles the visibility of a vertically stacked navigation menu.

1. **Mobile-Friendly Design**:
   - Use stacked layouts and toggleable menus for small screens.
2. **CSS Dropdowns and Hamburger Menus**:

o   Build navigation systems that adapt to different screen sizes.

3. **Interactivity**:

o   Enhance navigation with JavaScript for dynamic behaviors.

4. **Practical Example**:

o   The responsive menu for a restaurant demonstrates combining CSS and JavaScript for real-world applications.

In the next chapter, we'll explore **Using CSS Transitions and Animations**, learning how to add engaging effects to elevate your web designs. Let's bring some motion to your responsive layouts!

# CHAPTER 13: USING CSS TRANSITIONS AND ANIMATIONS

Motion effects, powered by CSS transitions and animations, add an engaging and interactive dimension to web design. Smooth hover effects, animated buttons, and subtle page transitions can enhance user experience by providing visual feedback and guiding user interactions. This chapter introduces CSS transitions, keyframes for animations, and practical techniques for adding motion effects, culminating in a real-world example of hover effects for buttons and links.

## Basics of CSS Transitions

CSS transitions allow smooth changes to an element's properties over a defined period. Transitions enhance interactions by replacing abrupt changes with visually appealing animations.

## *Key Transition Properties*

1. **transition-property**:
   - o Specifies which CSS properties should be animated.
   - o **Example**:

   css
   Copy code
   ```css
   button {
       transition-property: background-color, transform;
   }
   ```

2. **transition-duration**:
   - o Defines how long the transition takes.
   - o **Example**:

   css
   Copy code
   ```css
   button {
       transition-duration: 0.3s; /* 300 milliseconds */
   }
   ```

3. **transition-timing-function**:

- o Controls the speed curve of the transition.
- o Common values:
  - **ease**: Starts slow, speeds up, then slows down (default).
  - **linear**: Uniform speed throughout.
  - **ease-in**: Accelerates at the start.
  - **ease-out**: Decelerates at the end.
  - **ease-in-out**: Accelerates and decelerates.
- o **Example**:

css

Copy code

```
button {
  transition-timing-function: ease-in-out;
}
```

4. **transition-delay** (optional):
   - o Adds a delay before the transition starts.
   - o **Example**:

css

Copy code

```
button {
  transition-delay: 0.2s;
}
```

*Shorthand Syntax*

Combine all properties in one line:

css
Copy code
```css
button {
  transition: background-color 0.3s ease-in-out, transform 0.2s ease;
}
```

## Keyframes for Animations with @keyframes

The @keyframes rule defines animations by specifying key states (percentages) and the corresponding CSS properties.

### Basic Syntax

css
Copy code
```css
@keyframes animation-name {
  0% {
    property: value;
  }
  100% {
    property: value;
  }
}
```

### Applying Animations

Use the animation property to apply keyframes to an element.

**Example**:

css

Copy code

```
button {
  animation: bounce 1s ease-in-out infinite;
}


@keyframes bounce {
  0%, 100% {
    transform: translateY(0);
  }
  50% {
    transform: translateY(-10px);
  }
}
```

### *Key Animation Properties*

1. **animation-name**:
   - Specifies the name of the @keyframes animation.
2. **animation-duration**:
   - Defines how long the animation lasts.
3. **animation-timing-function**:
   - Controls the speed curve (same options as transitions).

4. **animation-delay**:
   - o  Adds a delay before the animation starts.

5. **animation-iteration-count**:
   - o  Number of times the animation runs (e.g., 1, 2, infinite).

6. **animation-direction**:
   - o  Defines the direction of the animation (normal, reverse, alternate).

## *Shorthand Syntax*

Combine all properties in one line:

css

Copy code

```
button {
  animation: bounce 1s ease-in-out infinite alternate;
}
```

## Adding Motion Effects to Enhance User Experience

### *1. Hover Effects for Buttons*

Use transitions to create subtle animations when a user hovers over a button.

**Example**:

css

Copy code

```css
button {
  padding: 10px 20px;
  background-color: #007bff;
  color: white;
  border: none;
  border-radius: 5px;
  cursor: pointer;
  transition: background-color 0.3s ease, transform 0.3s ease;
}

button:hover {
  background-color: #0056b3;
  transform: scale(1.1); /* Slightly enlarges the button */
}
```

## 2. Highlighting Links

Add animations to links that change color or underline on hover.

**Example**:

css

Copy code

```css
a {
  text-decoration: none;
  color: #007bff;
  position: relative;
```

```css
  transition: color 0.3s ease;
}

a:hover {
  color: #0056b3;
}

a::after {
  content: '';
  position: absolute;
  width: 0;
  height: 2px;
  bottom: -2px;
  left: 0;
  background-color: #0056b3;
  transition: width 0.3s ease;
}

a:hover::after {
  width: 100%; /* Creates an underline effect */
}
```

### 3. Animating Icons

Use keyframes to add looping animations to icons.

**Example**:

css
Copy code

```css
.icon {
  font-size: 24px;
  animation: spin 2s linear infinite;
}

@keyframes spin {
  0% {
    transform: rotate(0deg);
  }
  100% {
    transform: rotate(360deg);
  }
}
```

**Real-World Example: Hover Effects for Buttons and Links**

*HTML:*

html
Copy code

```html
<!DOCTYPE html>
<html lang="en">
<head>
```

```html
<meta charset="UTF-8">
<meta name="viewport" content="width=device-width, initial-scale=1.0">
<title>CSS Hover Effects</title>
<link rel="stylesheet" href="styles.css">
</head>
<body>
  <header>
    <h1>Welcome to Our Website</h1>
    <a href="#learn-more" class="link">Learn More</a>
    <button class="btn">Get Started</button>
  </header>
</body>
</html>
```

**CSS (styles.css):**

css

Copy code

```css
/* General Styles */
body {
  font-family: Arial, sans-serif;
  text-align: center;
  margin: 0;
  padding: 20px;
}
```

```css
header {
  padding: 50px 0;
}

/* Link Styles */
.link {
  text-decoration: none;
  color: #007bff;
  position: relative;
  font-size: 1.2rem;
  transition: color 0.3s ease;
}

.link:hover {
  color: #0056b3;
}

.link::after {
  content: ";
  position: absolute;
  width: 0;
  height: 2px;
  bottom: -2px;
  left: 0;
  background-color: #0056b3;
```

```css
  transition: width 0.3s ease;
}

.link:hover::after {
  width: 100%;
}

/* Button Styles */
.btn {
  padding: 10px 20px;
  background-color: #007bff;
  color: white;
  border: none;
  border-radius: 5px;
  cursor: pointer;
  font-size: 1rem;
  transition: background-color 0.3s ease, transform 0.3s ease;
}

.btn:hover {
  background-color: #0056b3;
  transform: scale(1.1);
}
```

*Result*

1. **Hover Effects for Buttons**:
   - Buttons change color and slightly enlarge when hovered over.

2. **Animated Links**:
   - Links change color and display a smooth underline animation on hover.

1. **CSS Transitions**:
   - Create smooth changes for hover effects and interactivity.

2. **CSS Animations**:
   - Use @keyframes for more complex animations like bouncing or spinning.

3. **Enhancing UX**:
   - Motion effects improve user engagement and feedback.

4. **Practical Example**:
   - Hover effects for buttons and links demonstrate real-world applications of transitions and animations.

In the next chapter, we'll explore **Building Responsive Forms**, focusing on creating user-friendly, accessible forms that adapt to different screen sizes. Let's make your forms beautiful and functional!

# CHAPTER 14: ENHANCING DESIGN WITH CSS VARIABLES

CSS variables, also known as custom properties, bring flexibility and maintainability to your stylesheets. They allow you to define reusable values, making it easier to update and manage consistent designs across your project. In this chapter, we'll explore how to declare and use CSS variables, create thematic designs, debug and maintain variable-based stylesheets, and implement a real-world example of a dark mode toggle using CSS variables.

## Declaring and Using Custom Properties

CSS variables are declared using the -- prefix and accessed with the var() function.

### 1. Declaring Variables

Variables are typically defined within the :root pseudo-class, making them globally accessible.

**Example**:

css
Copy code

```
:root {
  --primary-color: #007bff;
  --secondary-color: #6c757d;
  --font-size-base: 16px;
}
```

### 2. Using Variables

Use the var() function to reference variables.

**Example**:

css
Copy code

```
button {
  background-color: var(--primary-color);
  color: white;
```

```
font-size: var(--font-size-base);
padding: 10px 20px;
border: none;
border-radius: 5px;
}
```

### 3. Providing Fallback Values

Provide a fallback value in case a variable is undefined.

**Example**:

css

Copy code

```
button {
  color: var(--text-color, black); /* Defaults to black if --text-color
is not defined */
}
```

## Thematic Design with Reusable Variables

### 1. Creating a Theme

Define variables for a consistent theme, such as colors, fonts, and spacing.

**Example: Light Theme**:

css

Copy code

```css
:root {
  --background-color: #ffffff;
  --text-color: #000000;
  --link-color: #007bff;
}
```

**Example: Dark Theme**:

css

Copy code

```css
[data-theme="dark"] {
  --background-color: #121212;
  --text-color: #ffffff;
  --link-color: #bb86fc;
}
```

## 2. Applying the Theme

Use the variables across your styles to ensure consistency.

**Example**:

css

Copy code

```css
body {
  background-color: var(--background-color);
  color: var(--text-color);
}
```

```
a {
  color: var(--link-color);
  text-decoration: none;
}
```

### 3. Switching Themes Dynamically

Toggle themes by applying a data-theme attribute to the <html> or <body> element.

## Debugging and Maintaining Variable-Based Stylesheets

### 1. Debugging Variables

Use browser developer tools to inspect and debug CSS variables:

1. Open the **Elements** panel.
2. Select the element and check the Computed styles tab to view resolved variable values.

### 2. Overriding Variables

Variables can be redefined in specific scopes to apply contextual changes.

**Example**:

css
Copy code
.card {

```css
  --background-color: #f8f9fa; /* Overrides the global background color */
  background-color: var(--background-color);
}
```

### 3. *Organizing Variables*

Group variables by categories for better maintainability.

**Example**:

css
Copy code
```css
:root {
  /* Colors */
  --primary-color: #007bff;
  --secondary-color: #6c757d;

  /* Typography */
  --font-size-base: 16px;
  --font-family: Arial, sans-serif;

  /* Spacing */
  --padding-base: 10px;
  --margin-base: 10px;
}
```

## Real-World Example: Creating a Dark Mode Toggle Using CSS Variables

### *Goal*

Implement a toggle to switch between light and dark themes using CSS variables and JavaScript.

### *HTML:*

html

Copy code

```
<!DOCTYPE html>
<html lang="en">
<head>
  <meta charset="UTF-8">
  <meta name="viewport" content="width=device-width, initial-scale=1.0">
  <title>Dark Mode Toggle</title>
  <link rel="stylesheet" href="styles.css">
</head>
<body>
  <header>
    <h1>Dark Mode Example</h1>
    <button id="theme-toggle" aria-label="Toggle Dark Mode">Toggle Theme</button>
  </header>
  <main>
```

```
<p>This is a simple example of a dark mode toggle using CSS
variables.</p>
  </main>
  <script src="script.js"></script>
</body>
</html>
```

### CSS (styles.css):

css

Copy code

```
/* Light Theme (Default) */
:root {
  --background-color: #ffffff;
  --text-color: #000000;
  --button-bg: #007bff;
  --button-color: #ffffff;
}


/* Dark Theme */
[data-theme="dark"] {
  --background-color: #121212;
  --text-color: #ffffff;
  --button-bg: #bb86fc;
  --button-color: #121212;
}
```

```css
/* Global Styles */
body {
  background-color: var(--background-color);
  color: var(--text-color);
  font-family: Arial, sans-serif;
  margin: 0;
  padding: 20px;
}

button {
  background-color: var(--button-bg);
  color: var(--button-color);
  padding: 10px 20px;
  border: none;
  border-radius: 5px;
  cursor: pointer;
  transition: background-color 0.3s ease, color 0.3s ease;
}
```

***JavaScript (script.js):***

```javascript
javascript
Copy code
const toggleButton = document.getElementById('theme-toggle');
const body = document.body;
```

```
// Check and apply saved theme preference
const savedTheme = localStorage.getItem('theme');
if (savedTheme) {
  body.setAttribute('data-theme', savedTheme);
}


// Toggle between light and dark themes
toggleButton.addEventListener('click', () => {
  const currentTheme = body.getAttribute('data-theme');
  const newTheme = currentTheme === 'dark' ? 'light' : 'dark';

  body.setAttribute('data-theme', newTheme);
  localStorage.setItem('theme', newTheme); // Save preference
});
```

*Result*

1. **Default Theme**:
   - Light theme is applied on page load.
2. **Theme Toggle**:
   - Clicking the button toggles between light and dark themes.
3. **Persistent Preference**:
   - The user's theme preference is saved in local storage and reapplied on reload.

1. **CSS Variables**:
   o Simplify maintaining consistent styles across large projects.

2. **Dynamic Theming**:
   o Variables make it easy to create and switch between themes.

3. **Real-World Application**:
   o The dark mode toggle demonstrates combining CSS variables with JavaScript for interactive designs.

4. **Maintainability**:
   o Grouping and organizing variables improves readability and scalability of stylesheets.

In the next chapter, we'll explore **Responsive Grid Systems**, focusing on creating flexible layouts using CSS Grid and real-world examples like portfolio pages. Let's dive into advanced layout techniques!

# CHAPTER 15: RESPONSIVE FORMS

Forms are essential components of web design, enabling user interaction and data collection. Responsive forms ensure usability across devices, providing a seamless experience for all users. In this chapter, we'll explore how to style form elements, make them accessible, leverage HTML5 input types for responsiveness, and build a real-world example of a responsive contact form.

## Styling Form Inputs, Labels, and Buttons

Forms consist of various elements, including inputs, labels, and buttons. Consistent and intuitive styling improves usability and visual appeal.

## 1. Styling Form Inputs

Input fields should be styled for clarity and ease of use.

**Example**:

css
Copy code
```
input, textarea {
  width: 100%;
  padding: 10px;
  margin-bottom: 10px;
  border: 1px solid #ccc;
  border-radius: 5px;
  font-size: 16px;
  box-sizing: border-box; /* Ensures padding doesn't affect width */
}

input:focus, textarea:focus {
  border-color: #007bff;
  outline: none;
  box-shadow: 0 0 5px rgba(0, 123, 255, 0.5);
}
```

## 2. Styling Labels

Labels improve accessibility by clearly identifying form fields.

**Example**:

css
Copy code

```
label {
  font-weight: bold;
  display: block;
  margin-bottom: 5px;
}
```

### 3. Styling Buttons

Buttons should stand out and provide clear visual feedback.

**Example**:

css
Copy code

```
button {
  background-color: #007bff;
  color: white;
  border: none;
  padding: 10px 20px;
  border-radius: 5px;
  font-size: 16px;
  cursor: pointer;
  transition: background-color 0.3s ease;
```

```
}

button:hover {
  background-color: #0056b3;
}
```

## Making Forms Accessible and User-Friendly

Accessibility ensures forms are usable by everyone, including those with disabilities.

### 1. Associating Labels with Inputs

Use the for attribute on <label> to associate it with an input field's id.

**Example**:

html
Copy code
```
<label for="name">Name</label>
<input type="text" id="name" name="name" required>
```

### 2. Providing Descriptive Placeholders

Placeholders offer hints but should not replace labels.

**Example**:

html

Copy code

```
<input type="email" placeholder="Enter your email">
```

### 3. Using Fieldsets and Legends

Group related inputs with <fieldset> and <legend> for better organization and accessibility.

**Example**:

html

Copy code

```
<fieldset>
  <legend>Personal Information</legend>
  <label for="name">Name</label>
  <input type="text" id="name" name="name">
</fieldset>
```

### 4. Error Messaging

Use ARIA attributes (aria-invalid, aria-describedby) to indicate errors.

**Example**:

html

Copy code

```html
<input type="text" id="name" aria-invalid="true" aria-describedby="name-error">
<span id="name-error" role="alert">Name is required.</span>
```

## Using HTML5 Input Types and Attributes for Better Responsiveness

### *1. Input Types*

HTML5 introduces various input types for enhanced usability.

**Examples**:

- **email**: Ensures valid email format.

  html
  Copy code
  ```html
  <input type="email" required>
  ```

- **tel**: Optimized for numeric keypads on mobile devices.

  html
  Copy code
  ```html
  <input type="tel" pattern="[0-9]{10}" required>
  ```

- **number**: Provides a numeric input with step controls.

  html

Copy code

```
<input type="number" min="0" max="100">
```

- **date**: Provides a date picker.

html

Copy code

```
<input type="date">
```

## 2. Input Attributes

Attributes improve functionality and validation.

**Examples**:

- **required**: Makes fields mandatory.

html

Copy code

```
<input type="text" required>
```

- **pattern**: Specifies a regex for input validation.

html

Copy code

```
<input type="text" pattern="[A-Za-z]+" title="Only letters
are allowed.">
```

- **maxlength**: Limits the number of characters.

html

Copy code

```
<input type="text" maxlength="50">
```

## Real-World Example: Designing a Responsive Contact Form

### *HTML:*

html

Copy code

```
<!DOCTYPE html>
<html lang="en">
<head>
  <meta charset="UTF-8">
  <meta name="viewport" content="width=device-width, initial-scale=1.0">
  <title>Responsive Contact Form</title>
  <link rel="stylesheet" href="styles.css">
</head>
<body>
  <main>
    <h1>Contact Us</h1>
    <form class="contact-form" action="/submit" method="post">
     <fieldset>
      <legend>Personal Information</legend>
      <label for="name">Name</label>
```

```html
    <input       type="text"       id="name"       name="name"
placeholder="Your full name" required>
    <label for="email">Email</label>
    <input       type="email"       id="email"       name="email"
placeholder="Your email address" required>
    <label for="message">Message</label>
    <textarea   id="message"   name="message"   rows="5"
placeholder="Your message" required></textarea>
  </fieldset>
  <button type="submit">Submit</button>
  </form>
 </main>
</body>
</html>
```

***CSS (styles.css):***

css

Copy code

```css
/* General Styles */
body {
  font-family: Arial, sans-serif;
  margin: 0;
  padding: 20px;
  background-color: #f4f4f4;
}
```

```css
main {
  max-width: 600px;
  margin: 0 auto;
  background: white;
  padding: 20px;
  border-radius: 8px;
  box-shadow: 0 4px 6px rgba(0, 0, 0, 0.1);
}

h1 {
  text-align: center;
  margin-bottom: 20px;
}

/* Form Styles */
.contact-form fieldset {
  border: none;
  margin-bottom: 20px;
}

.contact-form label {
  display: block;
  font-weight: bold;
  margin-bottom: 5px;
```

```
}

.contact-form input,
.contact-form textarea {
  width: 100%;
  padding: 10px;
  margin-bottom: 10px;
  border: 1px solid #ccc;
  border-radius: 5px;
  font-size: 16px;
  box-sizing: border-box;
}

.contact-form input:focus,
.contact-form textarea:focus {
  border-color: #007bff;
  outline: none;
  box-shadow: 0 0 5px rgba(0, 123, 255, 0.5);
}

.contact-form button {
  width: 100%;
  padding: 10px;
  background-color: #007bff;
  color: white;
```

```
border: none;
border-radius: 5px;
font-size: 16px;
cursor: pointer;
transition: background-color 0.3s ease;
}


.contact-form button:hover {
background-color: #0056b3;
}
```

## *Result*

1. **Responsive Design**:
   o The form adjusts to different screen sizes, maintaining usability and readability.
2. **Accessibility**:
   o Labels are associated with inputs, and the form is keyboard- and screen-reader-friendly.
3. **Modern Features**:
   o HTML5 input types and attributes ensure better validation and responsiveness.


1. **Styling Forms**:

o   Consistent and intuitive design enhances usability.

2.  **Accessibility**:

    o   Labels, fieldsets, and error messaging improve form usability for all users.

3.  **HTML5 Features**:

    o   Modern input types and attributes simplify validation and responsiveness.

4.  **Practical Application**:

    o   The contact form demonstrates combining styling, accessibility, and responsiveness for real-world scenarios.

In the next chapter, we'll explore **Advanced CSS Grid Layouts**, delving into grid areas, alignment, and creating complex layouts like dashboards and portfolios. Let's continue mastering responsive design!

# CHAPTER 16: ADVANCED CSS TECHNIQUES

CSS offers powerful tools to create dynamic and visually appealing web designs. In this chapter, we explore advanced techniques such as pseudo-classes and pseudo-elements, combining selectors for complex styles, and using advanced properties like clip-path and filter. We'll conclude with a real-world example of a modern card design that leverages these advanced CSS features.

## Pseudo-Classes and Pseudo-Elements

Pseudo-classes and pseudo-elements allow you to target specific states or parts of elements without modifying the HTML.

### 1. Pseudo-Classes

Pseudo-classes define the state of an element, such as when it's hovered, focused, or a child of another element.

**Common Examples**:

- **:hover**: Applies styles when an element is hovered.

  css
  Copy code
  ```css
  button:hover {
    background-color: #007bff;
    color: white;
  }
  ```

- **:nth-child(n)**: Targets the nth child of a parent element.

  css
  Copy code
  ```css
  li:nth-child(2) {
    color: red;
  }
  ```

- **:focus**: Applies styles when an element is focused (e.g., an input field).

css

Copy code

```
input:focus {
  border-color: #007bff;
}
```

## 2. Pseudo-Elements

Pseudo-elements style specific parts of an element, such as the first letter or line of text.

**Common Examples:**

- **::before and ::after**: Add content or decorative elements before or after an element's content.

  css

  Copy code

  ```
  h1::before {
    content: "★ ";
    color: gold;
  }
  ```

- **::first-letter**: Style the first letter of a block of text.

  css

  Copy code

```css
p::first-letter {
  font-size: 2em;
  font-weight: bold;
}
```

## Combining Selectors for Complex Styles

Selectors can be combined to create more precise targeting for styling.

### 1. Descendant Selector

Targets elements nested within other elements.

css
Copy code
```css
article p {
  color: gray;
}
```

### 2. Adjacent Sibling Selector

Targets an element immediately following another.

css
Copy code
```css
h1 + p {
  font-size: 1.2em;
}
```

### 3. Attribute Selectors

Targets elements based on attributes or attribute values.

css

Copy code

```
input[type="text"] {
  border: 1px solid #ccc;
}
```

### 4. Grouping Selectors

Apply the same styles to multiple selectors.

css

Copy code

```
h1, h2, h3 {
  color: #333;
}
```

## Advanced Properties: clip-path and filter

### 1. clip-path

The clip-path property creates custom shapes for elements, enhancing visual design.

## Example: Clipping an Image:

css

Copy code

```
img {
  clip-path: circle(50% at 50% 50%);
```

}

## Shapes Supported:

- circle(): Circular shapes.
- polygon(): Custom polygonal shapes.
- inset(): Rectangular shapes with inset values.

### . *filter*

The filter property applies visual effects like blur, brightness, or grayscale to elements.

## Example: Applying a Blur:

css
Copy code
```
img {
  filter: blur(5px);
}
```

## Common Filters:

- blur(px): Blurs the element.
- brightness(%): Adjusts brightness.
- grayscale(%): Converts the element to grayscale.
- drop-shadow(offset-x offset-y blur-radius color): Adds a shadow.

**Real-World Example: Creating a Modern Card Design**

*Goal*

Design a visually appealing card using pseudo-elements, advanced selectors, and properties like clip-path and filter.

*HTML:*

html

Copy code

```
<!DOCTYPE html>
<html lang="en">
<head>
  <meta charset="UTF-8">
  <meta name="viewport" content="width=device-width, initial-scale=1.0">
  <title>Modern Card Design</title>
  <link rel="stylesheet" href="styles.css">
</head>
<body>
  <div class="card">
    <div class="card-image"></div>
    <div class="card-content">
      <h2>Modern Card</h2>
      <p>This is an example of a modern card design using advanced CSS techniques.</p>
```

```
    <button>Learn More</button>
  </div>
 </div>
</body>
</html>
```

## CSS (styles.css):

css

Copy code

```
/* General Reset */
* {
  margin: 0;
  padding: 0;
  box-sizing: border-box;
}

body {
  font-family: Arial, sans-serif;
  display: flex;
  justify-content: center;
  align-items: center;
  min-height: 100vh;
  background-color: #f4f4f4;
}
```

```css
/* Card Styles */
.card {
  position: relative;
  width: 300px;
  background: white;
  border-radius: 15px;
  overflow: hidden;
  box-shadow: 0 10px 15px rgba(0, 0, 0, 0.1);
  transform: translateY(0);
  transition: transform 0.3s ease;
}

.card:hover {
  transform: translateY(-10px);
}

/* Card Image */
.card-image {
  height: 200px;
  background:              url('https://via.placeholder.com/300x200')
center/cover no-repeat;
  clip-path: polygon(0 0, 100% 0, 100% 85%, 0 100%);
}

/* Card Content */
```

```css
.card-content {
  padding: 20px;
}


.card-content h2 {
  font-size: 1.5rem;
  margin-bottom: 10px;
  position: relative;
}


.card-content h2::after {
  content: ";
  display: block;
  width: 50px;
  height: 3px;
  background-color: #007bff;
  margin-top: 5px;
}


.card-content p {
  color: #666;
  font-size: 0.9rem;
  margin-bottom: 20px;
}
```

```
/* Button */
.card-content button {
  background-color: #007bff;
  color: white;
  border: none;
  padding: 10px 15px;
  border-radius: 5px;
  font-size: 1rem;
  cursor: pointer;
  transition: background-color 0.3s ease, transform 0.3s ease;
}

.card-content button:hover {
  background-color: #0056b3;
  transform: scale(1.1);
}
```

## *Result*

1. **Card Design**:
   - Features a clipped header image and a hover effect that lifts the card.
2. **Interactive Button**:
   - The button scales and changes color when hovered.
3. **Modern Touch**:

o Subtle use of clip-path, pseudo-elements, and transitions elevates the design.

**Key Takeaways**

1. **Pseudo-Classes and Pseudo-Elements**:
   o Enhance interactivity and create decorative effects without additional HTML.

2. **Advanced Selectors**:
   o Combine selectors for precise targeting and modular styles.

3. **Advanced Properties**:
   o Use clip-path and filter for unique visual effects.

4. **Practical Application**:
   o The modern card design demonstrates how advanced techniques can create visually stunning and interactive components.

In the next chapter, we'll explore **Responsive Grid Systems**, focusing on building flexible and scalable layouts with CSS Grid and real-world examples like portfolio pages. Let's dive deeper into layout mastery!

# CHAPTER 17: INTRODUCTION TO RESPONSIVE FRAMEWORKS

Responsive frameworks like Bootstrap and Tailwind CSS simplify web design by offering pre-built styles, components, and layout systems that adapt to different screen sizes. This chapter explores the fundamentals of responsive frameworks, focusing on grid systems, customization, and a real-world example of rebuilding a simple website using Bootstrap.

## Overview of Popular Frameworks

### 1. Bootstrap

Bootstrap is a widely used front-end framework with a comprehensive set of pre-designed components and a powerful grid system.

**Key Features**:

- Mobile-first responsive design.
- Grid layout system using rows and columns.
- Extensive library of components like buttons, modals, and forms.
- Customizable with Sass and built-in utility classes.

**Example**:

html
Copy code

```html
<div class="container">
  <div class="row">
    <div class="col-md-6">Column 1</div>
    <div class="col-md-6">Column 2</div>
  </div>
</div>
```

## 2. Tailwind CSS

Tailwind CSS is a utility-first framework, offering low-level utility classes for creating custom designs.

**Key Features**:

- Utility classes for spacing, typography, colors, and more.
- Highly customizable via a configuration file.
- No pre-designed components, providing design flexibility.

**Example**:

html
Copy code

```html
<div class="container mx-auto px-4">
  <div class="grid grid-cols-2 gap-4">
    <div class="p-4 bg-blue-500 text-white">Column 1</div>
    <div class="p-4 bg-green-500 text-white">Column 2</div>
  </div>
</div>
```

**Using Grid Systems in Frameworks**

Responsive frameworks rely heavily on grid systems for layout design. Grid systems divide the screen into rows and columns, making it easy to create flexible layouts.

*1. Bootstrap's Grid System*

Bootstrap uses a 12-column grid system.

**Example**:

html

Copy code

```
<div class="container">
 <div class="row">
  <div class="col-sm-4">Column 1</div>
  <div class="col-sm-4">Column 2</div>
  <div class="col-sm-4">Column 3</div>
 </div>
</div>
```

**Breakpoints**:

- col- (default): For extra small screens (<576px).
- col-sm-: For small screens (≥576px).
- col-md-: For medium screens (≥768px).
- col-lg-: For large screens (≥992px).
- col-xl-: For extra large screens (≥1200px).

## 2. Tailwind's Grid System

Tailwind's grid system uses utility classes for precise control.

**Example**:

html

Copy code

```
<div class="grid grid-cols-3 gap-4">
```

```
<div class="p-4 bg-blue-500">Column 1</div>
<div class="p-4 bg-green-500">Column 2</div>
<div class="p-4 bg-red-500">Column 3</div>
</div>
```

## Customizing Frameworks for Unique Designs

Frameworks like Bootstrap and Tailwind CSS are highly customizable, allowing you to tailor styles to match your design requirements.

### 1. Customizing Bootstrap

- Modify the variables.scss file to adjust colors, spacing, and fonts.
- Use utility classes like text-primary or bg-light for quick customizations.

**Example**:

scss
Copy code
```scss
// Override Bootstrap variables
$primary: #007bff;
$secondary: #6c757d;

// Import Bootstrap styles
```

```
@import 'bootstrap';
```

## 2. Customizing Tailwind CSS

- Modify the tailwind.config.js file to define custom themes, colors, and breakpoints.

**Example**:

javascript
Copy code

```javascript
module.exports = {
  theme: {
    extend: {
      colors: {
        brand: {
          light: '#3ab0ff',
          DEFAULT: '#007bff',
          dark: '#0056b3',
        },
      },
    },
  },
};
```

## Real-World Example: Rebuilding a Simple Website Using Bootstrap

### *Scenario*

Rebuild a basic website layout with a header, main content, and footer using Bootstrap's responsive grid system.

### *HTML:*

html

Copy code

```
<!DOCTYPE html>
<html lang="en">
<head>
  <meta charset="UTF-8">
  <meta name="viewport" content="width=device-width, initial-scale=1.0">
  <title>Bootstrap Website</title>
  <link href="https://cdn.jsdelivr.net/npm/bootstrap@5.3.0-alpha3/dist/css/bootstrap.min.css" rel="stylesheet">
</head>
<body>
  <header class="bg-primary text-white text-center py-4">
   <h1>My Bootstrap Website</h1>
  </header>
```

```html
<main class="container my-5">
  <div class="row">
    <div class="col-md-8">
      <h2>Main Content</h2>
      <p>This is the main content area of the website.</p>
    </div>
    <div class="col-md-4 bg-light p-3">
      <h2>Sidebar</h2>
      <p>This is the sidebar with additional information.</p>
    </div>
  </div>
</main>


<footer class="bg-dark text-white text-center py-3">
  <p>© 2024 My Website</p>
</footer>
</body>
</html>
```

***CSS (Optional Customization):***

css

Copy code

```css
/* Override Bootstrap classes */
.bg-primary {
  background-color: #007bff !important;
```

```
}
```

```
.bg-dark {
  background-color: #333 !important;
}
```

## *Key Features*

1. **Header**:
   - Full-width header with a primary background color.
2. **Main Content**:
   - Two-column layout: an 8-column main content area and a 4-column sidebar.
3. **Footer**:
   - Full-width footer with a dark background color.

## *Result*

- The layout adjusts dynamically across screen sizes.
- On smaller screens, the sidebar stacks below the main content, ensuring responsiveness.

1. **Frameworks Simplify Design**:

- o Bootstrap and Tailwind CSS provide powerful tools for creating responsive websites quickly.

2. **Grid Systems**:
   - o Framework grid systems enable flexible and scalable layouts.

3. **Customization**:
   - o Frameworks can be tailored for unique designs with configuration files or custom styles.

4. **Practical Application**:
   - o Rebuilding a simple website demonstrates the power of Bootstrap for responsive web design.

In the next chapter, we'll dive into **Performance Optimization for Responsive Web Design**, focusing on techniques to improve load times and responsiveness. Let's ensure your designs are not only beautiful but also fast!

# CHAPTER 18: INTRODUCTION TO CSS PREPROCESSORS

CSS preprocessors like SASS (Syntactically Awesome Stylesheets) and LESS (Leaner Style Sheets) enhance the capabilities of vanilla CSS by introducing advanced features like variables, nesting, and mixins. These tools improve maintainability, scalability, and efficiency in writing stylesheets. In this chapter, we'll explore what preprocessors are, delve into key features of SASS, learn how to compile SASS into CSS, and build a reusable stylesheet using SASS.

## What Are Preprocessors Like SASS and LESS?

### CSS Preprocessors Overview

CSS preprocessors are scripting languages that extend CSS with additional functionality. They require a compilation step to convert the preprocessor code into standard CSS.

### *Benefits of Preprocessors*

1. **Variables**: Store reusable values like colors, font sizes, and spacing.
2. **Nesting**: Write cleaner, hierarchical CSS that mirrors HTML structure.
3. **Mixins**: Reuse blocks of styles with parameters for flexibility.
4. **Functions**: Perform calculations and transformations directly in your styles.
5. **Modularity**: Break styles into smaller, manageable files for better organization.

### *SASS vs. LESS*

- **SASS**:
  - More widely used and feature-rich.
  - Supports two syntaxes: .sass (indented) and .scss (CSS-like syntax).
- **LESS**:
  - Similar features but generally considered less powerful than SASS.
  - Written in a syntax closer to CSS.

**Comparison**:

| Feature | SASS | LESS |
|---|---|---|
| Syntax | SCSS/SASS | CSS-like |
| Variables | $variable | @variable |
| Community | Large | Smaller |

Compatibility Requires Ruby or Node.js Node.js only

**Variables, Mixins, and Nesting in SASS**

*1. Variables*

SASS variables store reusable values for colors, fonts, or sizes.

**Example**:

scss

Copy code

```scss
// Define variables
$primary-color: #007bff;
$secondary-color: #6c757d;
$font-stack: 'Arial', sans-serif;

// Use variables
body {
  font-family: $font-stack;
```

```scss
color: $primary-color;
}


button {
  background-color: $primary-color;
  color: $secondary-color;
}
```

## 2. Nesting

Nesting allows you to write hierarchical CSS that mirrors the structure of your HTML, reducing repetitive selectors.

**Example**:

scss
Copy code

```scss
nav {
  ul {
    list-style: none;
    li {
      display: inline-block;
      a {
        text-decoration: none;
        color: $primary-color;
      }
    }
```

```
  }
}
```

**Compiles to**:

css
Copy code
```
nav ul {
  list-style: none;
}

nav ul li {
  display: inline-block;
}

nav ul li a {
  text-decoration: none;
  color: #007bff;
}
```

## 3. Mixins

Mixins allow you to define reusable blocks of styles with optional parameters.

**Example**:

scss

Copy code

```
@mixin button-style($bg-color, $text-color) {
  background-color: $bg-color;
  color: $text-color;
  padding: 10px 20px;
  border: none;
  border-radius: 5px;
  cursor: pointer;
}


button.primary {
  @include button-style($primary-color, white);
}


button.secondary {
  @include button-style($secondary-color, black);
}
```

## Compiling SASS into CSS

### 1. Installation

Install SASS using npm or a preprocessor GUI tool.

bash

Copy code

npm install -g sass

## 2. Compiling

Use the sass command to compile SASS/SCSS files into CSS.

**Example**:

bash

Copy code

sass styles.scss styles.css

## 3. Watching Files

Automatically recompile files when changes are made.

bash

Copy code

sass --watch styles.scss:styles.css

## Real-World Example: Building a Reusable Stylesheet with SASS

### Scenario

Create a reusable SASS stylesheet for a website with consistent design elements like colors, buttons, and typography.

### File Structure:

plaintext

Copy code

styles/

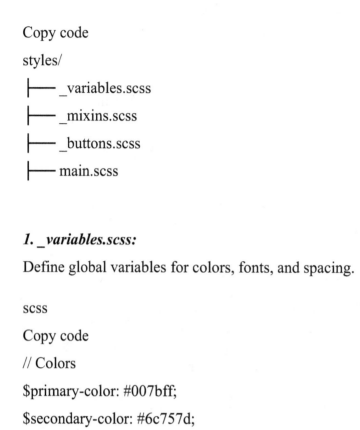

```
styles/
├── _variables.scss
├── _mixins.scss
├── _buttons.scss
├── main.scss
```

## 1. _variables.scss:

Define global variables for colors, fonts, and spacing.

scss

Copy code

```scss
// Colors
$primary-color: #007bff;
$secondary-color: #6c757d;
$text-color: #333;

// Typography
$font-stack: 'Arial', sans-serif;

// Spacing
$padding-base: 10px;
```

## 2. _mixins.scss:

Create reusable mixins for common styles.

scss

Copy code

```scss
@mixin flex-center {
  display: flex;
  justify-content: center;
  align-items: center;
}


@mixin responsive($breakpoint) {
  @media (min-width: $breakpoint) {
    @content;
  }
}
```

### 3. _buttons.scss:

Style buttons using variables and mixins.

scss

Copy code

```scss
button {
  @include flex-center;
  padding: $padding-base $padding-base * 2;
  border: none;
  border-radius: 5px;
  cursor: pointer;
```

```scss
  font-family: $font-stack;
  font-size: 1rem;

  &.primary {
    background-color: $primary-color;
    color: white;
  }

  &.secondary {
    background-color: $secondary-color;
    color: black;
  }
}
```

### 4. *main.scss:*

Import partials and compile them into a single stylesheet.

scss
Copy code

```scss
@import 'variables';
@import 'mixins';
@import 'buttons';

body {
  font-family: $font-stack;
```

```scss
  color: $text-color;
  margin: 0;
  padding: 0;
}

header {
  @include flex-center;
  background-color: $primary-color;
  color: white;
  padding: $padding-base;
}
```

**Compiled CSS (main.css):**

css

Copy code

```css
body {
  font-family: 'Arial', sans-serif;
  color: #333;
  margin: 0;
  padding: 0;
}

header {
  display: flex;
  justify-content: center;
```

```css
  align-items: center;
  background-color: #007bff;
  color: white;
  padding: 10px;
}

button {
  display: flex;
  justify-content: center;
  align-items: center;
  padding: 10px 20px;
  border: none;
  border-radius: 5px;
  cursor: pointer;
  font-family: 'Arial', sans-serif;
  font-size: 1rem;
}

button.primary {
  background-color: #007bff;
  color: white;
}

button.secondary {
  background-color: #6c757d;
```

```
  color: black;

}
```

## Key Takeaways

1. **CSS Preprocessors**:
   - o Tools like SASS extend CSS capabilities, making stylesheets more maintainable and scalable.

2. **SASS Features**:
   - o Variables, nesting, and mixins streamline code and reduce duplication.

3. **Compilation**:
   - o SASS must be compiled into standard CSS for browsers to use.

4. **Real-World Application**:
   - o Reusable stylesheets improve design consistency and efficiency in larger projects.

In the next chapter, we'll explore **CSS Animation Frameworks**, learning how tools like Animate.css can simplify adding motion to your designs. Let's bring your projects to life!

# CHAPTER 19: ACCESSIBILITY IN RESPONSIVE DESIGN

Web accessibility ensures that websites are usable by everyone, including people with disabilities. When integrated with responsive design principles, accessibility enhances user experience across devices and platforms. This chapter covers the core principles of web accessibility, the role of semantic HTML and ARIA, tools for testing accessibility, and a real-world example of improving accessibility for a responsive webpage.

**Principles of Web Accessibility (WCAG)**

The **Web Content Accessibility Guidelines (WCAG)** outline standards for creating accessible websites. These guidelines are based on four principles: **Perceivable, Operable, Understandable, and Robust (POUR).**

## *1. Perceivable*

Content must be presented in ways that users can perceive:

- Provide text alternatives for non-text content.
- Ensure sufficient contrast between text and background.
- Use captions for multimedia.

## *2. Operable*

Users must be able to interact with the interface:

- Make all functionality accessible via keyboard.
- Provide enough time for users to complete tasks.
- Avoid content that causes seizures (e.g., flashing animations).

## *3. Understandable*

Content and navigation must be easy to understand:

- Use clear and consistent layouts.
- Provide input assistance for forms (e.g., error messages, instructions).

## *4. Robust*

Content must be compatible with various user agents, including assistive technologies:

- Use clean, valid HTML.
- Ensure compatibility with screen readers.

## Semantic HTML and ARIA Roles

### 1. Semantic HTML

Semantic elements convey the structure of a webpage, making it easier for assistive technologies to interpret content.

**Examples of Semantic Elements**:

- <header>: Represents a page or section header.
- <main>: Represents the main content of a page.
- <article>: Represents a self-contained piece of content.
- <footer>: Represents a footer for a section or page.

**Example**:

html
Copy code

```
<header>
  <h1>Website Title</h1>
  <nav>
   <ul>
    <li><a href="#home">Home</a></li>
    <li><a href="#about">About</a></li>
    <li><a href="#contact">Contact</a></li>
   </ul>
```

```
</nav>
</header>
```

## 2. ARIA Roles

ARIA (Accessible Rich Internet Applications) attributes enhance accessibility by providing additional context for dynamic elements.

**Common ARIA Roles**:

- role="navigation": Identifies navigation regions.
- role="button": Enhances interactivity for non-standard buttons.
- aria-label: Provides a label for elements without visible text.

**Example**:

html
Copy code

```html
<div role="navigation" aria-label="Main Menu">
  <button role="button" aria-expanded="false" aria-controls="menu">Menu</button>
  <ul id="menu" hidden>
    <li><a href="#home">Home</a></li>
    <li><a href="#about">About</a></li>
  </ul>
</div>
```

### Testing for Accessibility with Browser Tools

*1. Accessibility Features in Developer Tools*

Modern browsers include built-in tools for accessibility testing:

- **Chrome DevTools**:
  - Open the **Elements** panel.
  - Use the **Accessibility** tab to inspect ARIA roles, labels, and hierarchy.
- **Lighthouse**:
  - Run an accessibility audit to identify issues like color contrast or missing labels.

*2. Third-Party Tools*

- **WAVE**: Evaluates accessibility issues visually.
- **Axe DevTools**: Provides detailed reports on accessibility violations.
- **Screen Readers**:
  - Use tools like NVDA (Windows) or VoiceOver (Mac) to test screen reader compatibility.

*3. Key Areas to Test*

- **Keyboard Navigation**:

- o Ensure all interactive elements (e.g., links, buttons) are accessible via Tab.
- **Color Contrast**:
  - o Use contrast ratio tools to verify compliance with WCAG guidelines.
- **Labels and ARIA Attributes**:
  - o Check if all form inputs and interactive elements are appropriately labeled.

## Real-World Example: Improving Accessibility for a Responsive Webpage

### Scenario

We'll improve the accessibility of a responsive webpage with a navigation menu and a contact form.

### HTML:

html
Copy code

```
<!DOCTYPE html>
<html lang="en">
<head>
  <meta charset="UTF-8">
  <meta name="viewport" content="width=device-width, initial-scale=1.0">
  <title>Accessible Webpage</title>
```

```
  <link rel="stylesheet" href="styles.css">
</head>
<body>
 <header>
  <h1>My Website</h1>
  <nav>
    <button    id="menu-toggle"    aria-expanded="false"    aria-
controls="main-menu">Menu</button>
    <ul id="main-menu" role="menu" hidden>
     <li><a href="#home" role="menuitem">Home</a></li>
     <li><a href="#about" role="menuitem">About</a></li>
     <li><a href="#contact" role="menuitem">Contact</a></li>
    </ul>
  </nav>
 </header>

 <main>
  <section id="contact">
   <h2>Contact Us</h2>
   <form>
     <label for="name">Name</label>
     <input    type="text"    id="name"    name="name"    aria-
required="true">

     <label for="email">Email</label>
```

```html
        <input    type="email"    id="email"    name="email"    aria-
required="true">

        <button type="submit">Submit</button>
      </form>
    </section>
  </main>
</body>
</html>
```

***CSS (styles.css):***

css

Copy code

```css
/* General Styles */
body {
  font-family: Arial, sans-serif;
  line-height: 1.6;
  margin: 0;
  padding: 0;
}

header {
  background-color: #333;
  color: white;
  padding: 10px 20px;
}
```

```css
nav ul {
  list-style: none;
  padding: 0;
  margin: 0;
}

nav ul li {
  margin: 5px 0;
}

button {
  background-color: #007bff;
  color: white;
  border: none;
  padding: 10px 15px;
  cursor: pointer;
  font-size: 1rem;
  border-radius: 5px;
}

button:focus {
  outline: 2px dashed #0056b3;
}
```

*JavaScript (script.js):*

javascript

Copy code

```javascript
const menuToggle = document.getElementById('menu-toggle');
const menu = document.getElementById('main-menu');

menuToggle.addEventListener('click', () => {
  const isExpanded = menuToggle.getAttribute('aria-expanded') === 'true';
  menuToggle.setAttribute('aria-expanded', !isExpanded);
  menu.hidden = isExpanded;
});
```

*Accessibility Features*

1. **Keyboard Accessibility**:
   - The Tab key navigates through all interactive elements.
   - The menu toggle updates dynamically with aria-expanded.
2. **Semantic HTML**:
   - <header>, <nav>, and <main> elements structure the content.
3. **Labels and Roles**:
   - Form inputs have descriptive labels, and the menu uses ARIA roles.

1. **Principles of Accessibility**:
   - ○ Follow WCAG guidelines for perceivable, operable, understandable, and robust content.

2. **Semantic HTML**:
   - ○ Use meaningful elements like <nav> and <header> to improve structure.

3. **ARIA Roles**:
   - ○ Enhance accessibility for dynamic elements with ARIA attributes.

4. **Testing Tools**:
   - ○ Use browser dev tools and third-party extensions to identify and resolve issues.

5. **Practical Application**:
   - ○ The example demonstrates how to integrate accessibility into a responsive webpage.

In the next chapter, we'll explore **Performance Optimization for Responsive Websites**, focusing on reducing load times and enhancing user experience. Let's ensure your designs are fast and efficient!

# CHAPTER 20: PERFORMANCE OPTIMIZATION FOR RESPONSIVE WEBSITES

Responsive websites must not only look good on all devices but also load quickly to provide an optimal user experience. Performance optimization ensures your designs are fast, efficient, and user-friendly. This chapter covers key techniques like minifying CSS and HTML, leveraging a Content Delivery Network (CDN), and optimizing images and fonts. We'll conclude with a real-world example of auditing and optimizing a website using Google Lighthouse.

## Minifying CSS and HTML

Minification removes unnecessary characters (e.g., spaces, comments) from your CSS and HTML files, reducing file sizes and improving load times.

### 1. Minifying CSS

Tools like CSSNano or Terser can minify CSS by removing whitespace, redundant selectors, and comments.

**Example**:

css
Copy code
```
/* Before Minification */
body {
  font-family: Arial, sans-serif;
  background-color: #fff; /* Default background */
}


/* After Minification */
body{font-family:Arial,sans-serif;background-color:#fff;}
```

### 2. Minifying HTML

HTML minifiers like HTMLMinifier strip unnecessary characters from HTML.

**Example**:

html

Copy code

```
<!-- Before Minification -->
<!DOCTYPE html>
<html lang="en">
 <head>
  <title>My Website</title>
 </head>
 <body>
  <h1>Welcome</h1>
 </body>
</html>
```

```
<!-- After Minification -->
<!DOCTYPE html><html lang="en"><head><title>My Website</title></head><body><h1>Welcome</h1></body></html>
```

***Automated Tools***

- Use build tools like Webpack, Gulp, or Grunt to automate minification during development.

## Using a Content Delivery Network (CDN)

A CDN distributes website assets (e.g., images, scripts, styles) across multiple geographically distributed servers. Visitors download resources from the nearest server, reducing latency and improving performance.

### Benefits of a CDN

1. **Faster Load Times**:
   - Assets are served from servers closest to the user.
2. **Reduced Server Load**:
   - Requests are distributed across multiple servers.
3. **Improved Availability**:
   - CDNs handle traffic spikes and mitigate downtime.

### Popular CDN Providers

- **Cloudflare**: Free and paid options for global content delivery.
- **AWS CloudFront**: Part of the AWS ecosystem for scalable performance.
- **Google Cloud CDN**: Optimized for Google Cloud-hosted applications.

### Implementation Example

To include Bootstrap via a CDN:

html

Copy code

```
<link href="https://cdn.jsdelivr.net/npm/bootstrap@5.3.0-alpha3/dist/css/bootstrap.min.css" rel="stylesheet">
```

## Optimizing Images and Fonts for Faster Load Times

### *1. Image Optimization*

Images are often the heaviest assets on a website. Optimizing them significantly improves performance.

**Techniques**:

- **Use Modern Formats**:
  - **WebP** or **AVIF** offers smaller file sizes than JPEG/PNG without compromising quality.
- **Compress Images**:
  - Use tools like TinyPNG or ImageOptim to reduce file sizes.
- **Responsive Images**:
  - Use srcset to serve appropriately sized images based on the user's device.

html

Copy code

```
<img src="image-small.jpg" srcset="image-large.jpg 1024w" sizes="(max-width: 1024px) 100vw, 50vw" alt="Example Image">
```

### *2. Font Optimization*

Web fonts can slow down page load times if not optimized.

**Techniques**:

- **Choose Fewer Fonts**:
  - Limit the number of font families and weights.
- **Use Variable Fonts**:
  - Combine multiple font weights/styles into a single file.
- **Preload Fonts**:
  - Use the <link rel="preload"> attribute to load fonts early.

html
Copy code
```
<link rel="preload" href="font.woff2" as="font" type="font/woff2" crossorigin="anonymous">
```

### Real-World Example: Auditing and Optimizing a Website with Google Lighthouse

*Scenario*

You have a responsive website with slow load times. Use Google Lighthouse to identify and resolve performance issues.

## Step 1: Auditing the Website

1. Open your website in Google Chrome.
2. Right-click and select **Inspect**.
3. Navigate to the **Lighthouse** tab.
4. Select the audit type (**Performance** is most relevant for speed optimizations).
5. Click **Generate Report**.

**Key Metrics in Lighthouse**:

- **First Contentful Paint (FCP)**: Time to load the first visual content.
- **Largest Contentful Paint (LCP)**: Time to load the largest visual content.
- **Cumulative Layout Shift (CLS)**: Measures visual stability during loading.

## Step 2: Analyzing the Results

- **Opportunities**: Areas where performance can be improved (e.g., image compression, reducing unused CSS).
- **Diagnostics**: Details about potential improvements (e.g., font loading times, render-blocking resources).

## Step 3: Implementing Improvements

1. **Optimize Images**:
   o Replace large PNG files with compressed WebP versions.

html

Copy code

```
<img src="image.webp" alt="Optimized Image">
```

2. **Minify CSS and JavaScript**:
   o Use build tools like Webpack or Gulp to minify assets.

bash

Copy code

```
npm install cssnano terser
```

3. **Use Lazy Loading**:
   o Defer loading offscreen images.

html

Copy code

```
<img src="image.jpg" loading="lazy" alt="Lazy Loaded Image">
```

4. **Preload Key Resources**:
   o Preload critical assets like fonts and hero images.

html

Copy code

```
<link rel="preload" href="hero.jpg" as="image">
```

5. **Enable Compression**:

   o Use server-side compression like Gzip or Brotli to reduce file sizes.

## Step 4: Re-auditing

Run the Lighthouse report again to verify improvements. Compare metrics like FCP, LCP, and overall performance scores.

1. **Minification**:

   o Reduces file sizes for CSS, HTML, and JavaScript to improve load times.

2. **CDN Usage**:

   o Delivers assets from servers closer to users, reducing latency.

3. **Image and Font Optimization**:

   o Use modern formats, compress assets, and preload critical resources for faster loading.

4. **Lighthouse Audits**:

   o Provides actionable insights to improve performance and measure progress.

In the next chapter, we'll explore **Future Trends in Web Design**, discussing topics like AI-driven personalization, progressive web apps, and advanced CSS features shaping the future of responsive design. Let's look ahead!

# CHAPTER 21: THE FUTURE OF RESPONSIVE WEB DESIGN

Responsive web design continues to evolve, driven by emerging technologies and best practices for scalability and adaptability. This chapter explores cutting-edge tools like CSS Houdini, container queries, and new CSS units, the increasing importance of design systems, tips for staying updated with trends, and a real-world example of modernizing a legacy website.

**Emerging Technologies in Responsive Web Design**

*1. CSS Houdini*

CSS Houdini allows developers to write custom CSS properties and access the rendering pipeline of the browser, enabling previously impossible styling capabilities.

**Key Features**:

- **Custom Properties**: Extend the power of variables with complex logic.
- **Paint API**: Create dynamic styles like gradients and patterns directly in CSS.
- **Layout API**: Define custom layouts beyond the default Flexbox or Grid.

**Example: Custom Paint with Houdini**:

javascript

Copy code

```javascript
if ('paintWorklet' in CSS) {
  CSS.paintWorklet.addModule('path-to-worklet.js');
}
```

## 2. Container Queries

Container queries enable styles to be applied based on the size of a container rather than the viewport, addressing a long-standing limitation of media queries.

**Why They Matter**:

- Responsive components adapt to their container size.
- Enhances modularity in design systems.

**Example**:

css

Copy code

```css
.container {
  container-type: inline-size;
}

.card {
  width: 100%;
}

@container (min-width: 500px) {
  .card {
    width: 50%;
  }
}
```

### 3. New CSS Units

The introduction of new units like lvh, lvw, svh, and svw addresses inconsistencies in viewport measurements caused by mobile browser interfaces.

**Key Units**:

- **lvh (Large Viewport Height)**: Excludes browser UI from the measurement.
- **svh (Small Viewport Height)**: Includes the browser UI, representing the smallest possible height.

**Example**:

css
Copy code

```
.hero {
  height: 100lvh; /* Ensures the hero section always fills the visible area */
}
```

## The Role of Design Systems in Scalable Projects

### 1. What Are Design Systems?

A design system is a collection of reusable components, guidelines, and tools that ensure consistency and scalability in large projects.

**Key Elements**:

- **Component Libraries**: Pre-designed, reusable UI components.
- **Style Guides**: Rules for typography, colors, and spacing.
- **Tokens**: Design properties stored as variables (e.g., colors, fonts).

## 2. Benefits of Design Systems

- **Consistency**: Ensures uniformity across pages and devices.
- **Efficiency**: Reduces development time with prebuilt components.
- **Scalability**: Supports large teams working on complex projects.

## 3. Implementing a Design System

Use tools like Storybook, Figma, or Material Design to create and manage design systems.

**Example**:

- **Tokens**:

scss
Copy code
$primary-color: #007bff;
$font-size-base: 16px;

- **Reusable Components**:

html
Copy code
<button class="btn btn-primary">Click Me</button>

**Tips for Staying Updated with Web Design Trends**

1. **Follow Web Design Blogs**:
   - Websites like Smashing Magazine, CSS-Tricks, and A List Apart provide updates on new tools and techniques.

2. **Participate in Communities**:
   - Join forums and communities like Reddit's r/web_design or dev.to to discuss trends and get inspiration.

3. **Explore Experimental Features**:
   - Use browsers like Chrome Canary to test experimental web technologies.

4. **Enroll in Web Design Courses**:
   - Platforms like Udemy, Coursera, and freeCodeCamp offer courses on the latest web design trends.

5. **Subscribe to Newsletters**:
   - Stay informed with newsletters like CSS Weekly or Frontend Focus.

**Real-World Example: Adapting a Legacy Website to Modern Standards**

*Scenario*

You're tasked with updating a legacy website built with outdated techniques to meet modern responsive design standards.

***Legacy HTML:***

html

Copy code

```
<!DOCTYPE html>
<html>
<head>
  <title>Legacy Website</title>
  <style>
    .container {
      width: 960px;
      margin: 0 auto;
    }
  </style>
</head>
<body>
  <div class="container">
    <h1>Welcome to My Website</h1>
    <p>This is a legacy design.</p>
  </div>
</body>
</html>
```

***Modernized HTML:***

html

Copy code

```html
<!DOCTYPE html>
<html lang="en">
<head>
  <meta charset="UTF-8">
  <meta name="viewport" content="width=device-width, initial-scale=1.0">
  <title>Modernized Website</title>
  <link rel="stylesheet" href="styles.css">
</head>
<body>
  <header>
    <h1>Welcome to My Website</h1>
  </header>
  <main>
    <section>
      <p>This website has been updated with modern responsive design techniques.</p>
    </section>
  </main>
  <footer>
    <p>© 2024 Modernized Website</p>
```

```
  </footer>
</body>
</html>
```

**Modernized CSS (styles.css):**

css

Copy code

```css
/* Global Reset */
* {
  margin: 0;
  padding: 0;
  box-sizing: border-box;
}

body {
  font-family: Arial, sans-serif;
  line-height: 1.6;
  color: #333;
  background-color: #f4f4f4;
  margin: 0;
}

header, main, footer {
  padding: 20px;
  margin: auto;
```

```
  max-width: 1200px;
}


header {
  background-color: #007bff;
  color: white;
  text-align: center;
}


footer {
  background-color: #333;
  color: white;
  text-align: center;
}
```

## *New Features Added*

1. **Responsive Layout**:
   o Used max-width instead of fixed width for fluid layouts.
2. **Viewport Meta Tag**:
   o Ensures the design adapts to different screen sizes.
3. **Modern CSS Techniques**:
   o Applied modern typography and color schemes for better readability.

1. **Emerging Technologies**:
   - Tools like CSS Houdini, container queries, and new units provide unparalleled flexibility in responsive design.

2. **Design Systems**:
   - Crucial for maintaining consistency and scalability in large projects.

3. **Stay Updated**:
   - Regularly explore new trends, tools, and experimental features.

4. **Practical Example**:
   - Modernizing a legacy website demonstrates how to apply new techniques to improve usability and responsiveness.

In the next chapter, we'll wrap up with **Practical Applications of Responsive Web Design**, summarizing key techniques and showcasing how to build end-to-end responsive projects. Let's bring it all together!

www.ingramcontent.com/pod-product-compliance
Lightning Source LLC
LaVergne TN
LVHW051443050326
832903LV00030BD/3213

* 9 7 9 8 3 0 0 8 3 1 0 8 0 *